GOOD VI

GOOD VIBRATIONS

The True Story Behind
Ann Summers

Jacqueline Gold

This paperback edition first published in Great Britain in 1996 by
Pavilion Books Limited
26 Upper Ground
London SE1 9PD

First published in hardback in 1995

Text designed by AB3

Jacket designed by The Bridgewater Book Company.
Jacket photograph © Brian Aris.

A CIP catalogue record for this book is available from the British Library

ISBN 1-85793-906-9

Printed and bound in Great Britain by Cox and Wyman, Reading
Typeset in 14½pt Bernhard Modern by Servis Filmsetting Ltd, Manchester

2 4 6 8 10 9 7 5 3 1

This book may be ordered by post direct from the publisher. Please
contact the Marketing Department. But try your bookshop first.

To my dad

'The only thing we have to fear is fear itself – nameless, unjustified terror which paralyses needed efforts to convert retreat into advance.'
Franklin D. Roosevelt, 4 March 1933

CONTENTS

PREFACE

I DECIDED TO WRITE THIS book because I felt it would provide a golden opportunity to set the record straight after years of encountering preconceived opinions about me and Ann Summers. As a woman working in the sex industry, I have found it rewarding and refreshing to be given the time and space to dispel some of these prejudices.

There are so many people that I want to thank for their help and encouragement over the years that I will be unable to name them all. But they know who they are and I offer them my sincerest gratitude. I was the most unlikely person ever to become a success and I hope this book provides inspiration to them and to others who have ideas and need the courage to act on them.

I owe my success chiefly to my father, David, because he treated me like everyone else – in fact probably a lot harder – and that was very character-building. He has also been a wealth of inspiration to me.

Vanessa, my sister, deserves a special note of thanks for being the best friend that anyone could ever hope to have. Since we became friends, I have known that I can rely on her for anything and her loyalty is second to none.

Julie Harris, my sales director, has given me massive support and dedication through the years and is truly motivating. The trust that has grown between us is such that we can confide anything in each other. My well-being and that of Ann Summers are in Julie's heart. She has always thought of what is best for me and the company through some very difficult situations and that has cemented us even closer together.

I would like to recognize the late Loretta Leese, one of our best unit organizers ever, who had such dedication to the company and showed such courage in the face of illness that she was an inspiration to us all.

I would also like to thank Wendy Holden, who helped me to write this book, and to acknowledge her expertise in extracting every secret and emotion out of people. I certainly told her things that I never thought I would tell anyone, and everyone who met her said the same. Working on this project together, we have become firm friends and realize that there are many parallels in our lives — even down to having the same coffee cups!

Wendy would like to thank Mark Lucas, whose smooth voice (we both agreed) should definitely feature on our best-selling Talking Vibrator. Special thanks to the wonderful Lavinia Barnes, whose calm reassurance in the face of adversity kept us all buoyant.

My thanks must also go to another exceptional person — my press officer, Jacquie Wilson. Her valuable work in the background during the writing of this book has always been with enthusiasm, optimism and a cheery smile.

Thanks must also go to my family — Dorothy, Derek, Tony and Stuart and, especially, my mum — for all their love and support. And I must finally thank all the women at Ann Summers, the executives in particular, for their determination and belief in the company in the face of all the prejudices they have encountered in the course of their working lives.

Chapter One
AWAKENINGS

SITTING IN A SMOKY ROOM full of women in a council flat in south-east London, trying to draw a picture of my husband's 'meat and two veg' on a piece of paper placed on top of my head, may not seem the most traditional way of becoming inspired to start a multi-million-pound business empire – but that is exactly how I got started.

It was spring 1981; I was twenty years old and earning about £50 a week as an office junior in my father's company. I had certainly never seen anything like the scene before me in that small flat in Thamesmead. Laughing women sat side by side, crammed together on sofas and on the floor, passing round lingerie and marital aids as if they were pieces of fruit at a street market. Naive for my age, tongue-tied and still painfully shy, I was both embarrassed and exhilarated by the enthusiasm surrounding me. I watched wide-eyed as the party organizer stirred the group of giggling women into a frenzy of hysteria as she produced the Double Dong – a double vibrator for the brave of heart. The screams of laughter could be heard throughout the tower block.

When the organizers introduced me as the daughter of the man who owned Ann Summers – then a chain of sex shops and a mail order business – the guests overwhelmed me with suggestions. This was such fun, they said. Why didn't Ann Summers organize their own parties? 'We want to buy sexy underwear for ourselves, but we wouldn't be seen dead in any of your shops,' one woman told me, a view I completely understood as I had already fought my way through the dirty mac brigade on a recent visit.

Carol, the party hostess, was delighted when her friends Chris Rogers and Ann Galea – both energetic organizers for a company called Pippa Dee, which held parties in hostesses' homes and sold clothes direct to their guests – decided to add to their range some goods bought wholesale from Ann Summers. 'It really spices the evening up,' she said; 'a bit of naughty but nice.' By now I knew exactly what she meant.

That night in Thamesmead I experienced an atmosphere that was totally new to me. As the organizers started chatting and relaxing with a cigarette, a glass of wine and a few sandwiches, I felt myself being carried along with the enthusiasm. All the young women were talking at the same time: it was the typical sort of atmosphere that you would expect in a close-knit community.

The party organizer was excellent: she set up party games – new to me, but commonly used to break the ice at Party Plan events. We were all told to write things down and then I found myself trying to draw my husband Tony's 'tackle'; I was very disappointed when, despite what I considered to be a creative streak, my best efforts did not win a prize. When it came to the presentation of the mostly red-and-black lace Ann Summers underwear, I had to stop myself getting my pen out to order something and remind myself that I had direct access to the products at work.

The Pippa Dee items were shown first and I remember thinking the clothes were rather boring – very much the C & A look, as it was then. But I was very interested in the conversations that started up as soon as the Ann Summers items came out. The lingerie and marital aids really seemed to make people open up spontaneously about their sex lives and relationships. I had never heard such topics discussed in public before.

I was at the party for a couple of hours, and all my early anxieties were soon calmed. I had been nervous about going there in the first place because I didn't know anyone and the council estate was miles from where I lived in Kent, but I loved the evening and was fascinated by all that I saw and heard, particularly when I began to realize that this idea could really take off with Ann Summers. Party Plan was a brilliant scheme, originally thought up in the 1950s by the Tupperware company in America and copied worldwide to sell anything from make-up and jewellery to environmentally sound cleaning products. There were few over-heads and you had direct access to cash customers. And I noticed that the ordering process could be re-structured in such a way that none of the women there would know what anyone else had ordered and neither could they find out. As the ordered goods were delivered to the customers' homes a few days later by the party organizer, it could all be very discreet.

There and then, my mind was made up and I decided to hold some parties myself. I knew I had to investigate the whole concept in more detail and see how it worked, but my head was a whirl, so fired up was I with the excitement of it all.

I arrived home late, but Tony had waited up for me and I couldn't stop talking about it all. I don't think I mentioned drawing his private parts in front of twelve strange women, but he realized roughly what was involved and was happy to see me so stimulated. He was aware that I wanted more from my life than menial office work, but I don't think he or anyone else realized how ambitious I was.

My ambition was my secret, and I didn't share it with anyone. Ever since my early teens I had been inspired by the idea of making money and becoming financially independent, and my recent brief experience of market stalls had me hooked on the idea of selling directly to the public. Tony, the hard-working, ambitious man whom I had married just a few months earlier, was an inspiration in a way too. I looked up to him because he had a good job as a diamond sorter at De Beers, but I was also aware that he was rather old-fashioned and traditional in many ways: I knew he wanted to settle down and have a family and a wife at home. His job was regular and he also had opportunities to go abroad, but he wanted to get on and always thought that he, not I, would run his own busi-ness.

But now my turn had come. I could hardly sleep that night for excitement. I think I knew, instinctively, that this was the way forward for me. Little did I guess how far it would take me, and Tony too.

Up until that point there had been nothing in my life to indicate anything other than an entirely unremarkable future. I had worked my way through a series of part-time and then full-time jobs, and my father certainly expected me to marry young and have children. He had resigned himself to the fact that there was no one to take over the growing business empire he and his brother Ralph had created from publishing and other interests. But I was going to prove him wrong.

Born Jacqueline Shirley Gold in Stone Park Nursing Home, Beckenham, Kent, at 6 lb 4 oz, on 16 July 1960 – Shirley after the midwife who was kind to my mother through a difficult birth – I was the eldest daughter of David Gold, an East End bricklayer, and his twenty-two-year-old wife, Beryl. My younger sister, Vanessa, affectionately known in the family as 'Nessy', arrived seven years later.

My parents had met through my mother's sister, Heather, and her boyfriend, Terry Green, my father's best friend, whom Heather eventually married. My parents had been married for two years before I was born, and right from the outset there were problems. My father had abandoned a career as a professional footballer because his father, Godfrey, known as 'Goddy' Gold, a market trader and wheeler dealer had refused to endorse the authorization papers for him to sign up with West Ham. 'Finish your apprentice-ship as a bricklayer first,' he had told him. 'One day you'll thank me for it.'

So for four years Dad laid bricks in the East End, a period he describes as the unhappiest of his life because he was poor, perma-nently cold and miserable. The only bright spot was playing foot-ball for 'boot money' (unofficial payments to players left in their boots) for Fulham, Leyton and Barking. He also played for London Youth against Glasgow Youth at Crystal Palace and scored the winning goal in the last ten minutes in front of 12,000 people. He describes it as the highlight of his young life.

Around the time that I was born, Goddy arrived at the building site in Bow where my father was working and shouted up the scaffolding to him: 'I've found a shop, son. Come on, let's go.' My father was delighted to tell his foreman to 'Lick 'em and stick 'em' (lick his employment stamps and stick them in the book), and off he went to work in my grandfather's newly acquired bookshop in Villier Street, Charing Cross, selling books, magazines and anything they thought might turn a profit. Dad's younger brother Ralph, then a national bantam weight boxing champion and an up-and-coming salesman for the Corona soft drinks company, joined them to make up 'The Three Musketeers'.

Goddy was the sort of man who had fingers in lots of pies. He was a typical East End businessman of that era, a lovable rogue who managed to dodge the war by claiming he suffered from hayfever. He and my grandmother, Rosie, were quite different to my mother's parents, who were old-fashioned and rather prudish. As a young man Goddy had been in and out of prison for fraud several times, including four years in Dartmoor.

Left alone and penniless with three children to bring up – Dad, Ralph and their baby sister Marie – my indomitable Grandma Rosie had rented a bomb-damaged Victorian terraced house in Upton Park, East London, and set up a stall outside her front window on which she initially sold buttons, books and comics. She also worked as a cook at a local café and scrubbed floors when the children were at school.

David and Ralph then helped her to convert her front bedroom into a shop and Rosie's Bookshop was up and running. When Goddy came out of prison and found Rosie making a living as a bookseller he decided to use his contacts at the East London docks to buy the books, magazines and comics that were thrown into the bottom of American container ships as ballast. They were largely detective and cowboy magazines, cartoon comics, karate manuals and puzzle books, but they also included top shelf girlie magazines, which Goddy soon discovered were in great demand. Poor old Rosie! She had to keep the shop going while Goddy launched himself into a career in the bingo halls and continued to pursue other women.

Later on, Goddy set up a company called Famé Perfumes. The perfumes smelled like the famous brand names, and their names and packaging were very similar, but they cost a fraction of the price. He sold them to anyone who wanted to buy – market traders or the men you see with suitcases in Oxford Street. It was all perfectly legitimate and he was never prosecuted for anything connected with Famé, but the London *Evening Standard* once ran an article entitled 'PORN BARONS BEHIND PERFUME PEDLARS' and he became quite a controversial figure.

Rosie still looks fabulous – slim and elegant and beautiful. Now in her eighties, she still works behind the counter at her shop in Upton Park, selling sweets and cards. She is also a great fan of West Ham United Football Club and goes to all the local matches. I don't see her nearly as often as I'd like. She refuses to give up work, even though Dad and Ralph have bought her a lovely flat and she has no more money worries, but she says the shop has always kept her going. I know I was inspired by the example of this fabulous independent woman, enjoying herself and really living life to the full. I certainly hope I look that good at eighty!

After he and Rosie separated, Goddy and his sons took on a few more bookshops and set up an office in Dock Street, near the Tower of London. They had shops in John Adam Street, near Charing Cross, in Angel Lane, Stratford, and another in the East India Dock Road, all three of which made them a lot of money when the local councils later bought them up for road-widening schemes. Marie ran the East India Dock Road site as a greetings card shop. Goddy was also still working the markets and gambling and had interests all over London, and by this time the family had started to produce 'girlie' magazines to compete with the new British titles like *Mayfair* and *Penthouse*.

Sadly, Dad and Ralph fell out with their father thirty years ago and the rift has never been healed. Contrary to what people sometimes write and say about him, my father is a man of very high principles and morals and he disapproved of some of the things my grandfather was trying to do. The rift was essentially a difference of opinion about the way the business was being run. They were fine as 'The Three Musketeers', with profits and shares being split three ways, until Dad and Ralph started to stand up to their father. Matters came to a head when Goddy wanted to buy £20,000 worth of stockings at a time when tights had just become all the rage and the company had cash flow problems. My father and Ralph objected but my grandfather went ahead anyway. When they challenged him he produced what he thought was his trump card, a secret document that gave him the controlling shares and the vote; it turned out to be worthless. The sons felt let down and started to drift away from Goddy. Then, in 1969, they relocated to a new warehouse at Whyteleafe in Surrey and didn't take him with them. They have hardly spoken since.

Strangely, for years afterwards the three-way split remained, and even though they weren't talking, they had to submit accounts and papers for signing by the other party. That meant, of course, that whenever Goddy did anything that made the news, my father and Ralph were dragged into it all again because their names were on the documents.

Goddy is in his seventies now and lives in a lovely house in Surrey. He is still a typical East Ender – he wears lots of gold rings and drives expensive cars. He also has another son, Mark, by a relationship he had with a seventeen-year-old girl. Mark is now in his early twenties and is a lovely man. Goddy's bitterness seems to be aimed more towards my father, the elder brother, than at Ralph. My father has done everything he possibly can to mend the terrible rift, and holds out his hand to my grandfather at weddings or funerals, but Goddy always turns his back on him. He refuses point blank to have any reconciliation. Instead he has devoted himself to Mark. He gave up the perfume business in the end and decided to open a string of opticians called Better Specs, in which Mark is involved.

My grandparents on my mother's side were called Percy and Lydia, but she was better known as 'Did'. They lived in Beckenham and then Shirley, until my grandfather died fifteen years ago after suffering several strokes. I was quite close to 'Did'. My sister and I used to visit her regularly at her home on Hayling Island until she died in 1994 at the age of eighty-nine.

I was a tiny little sparrow of a child – small and very clumsy. I was always at the hospital having stitches for this or that. I have a scar on my forehead from falling off my bike and another scar where I broke my fingers, just playing with a foot pump in the back of the car. My earliest memory involves an accident which occurred when I was about two. I was walking up my grandmother's garden path when, like something out of a slapstick comedy, I stepped on a garden rake which hit me in the face. On another occasion I fell off my bike and had to have stitches in my lip. I hated hospitals, I hated doctors and I hated dentists. I can remember being dragged screaming up the ramp to the hospital on that occasion. Mum always said I was a very quiet child except when I had to visit the doctor.

My mother was always extremely protective – overly protective – which could be very stifling at times. I was always desperate to break away. I was not allowed to go out and play with friends in case I got run over or kidnapped. She admits now that she was a little neurotic about us. Holidays were very boring: we never went anywhere exciting because Mum didn't like travelling. On the beach she used to draw an invisible 15-foot line in the sand around me and I wasn't to go beyond that.

I was allowed to have friends back to tea occasionally, but Mum became anxious if I went out and never allowed me to go on school trips or anything like that. She would give herself convincing reasons why I couldn't go. She was always a real worrier; she still is. She was also too nervous to fly – or allow us to – so my father, who loves flying (he has a pilot's licence and even owned Biggin Hill Flying Club for a time), was largely confined to holidays in Britain.

Mind you, sometimes those holidays gave us unexpected opportunities: once, when I was about eight, we went to the Atlantic Hotel in Newquay. I went on a lot of business trips with my parents and this was one of them. There were just the three of us there, so Vanessa must have stayed at home. One night, there was a terrible commotion – people outside were screaming and yelling. Then, after a while, everything went quiet. The next morning I was told that the Beatles had arrived at the hotel and were having a photo session on the lawn with all their girlfriends. My father proudly marched me out there and, before I knew it, he had the photographer taking two pictures of me – one on George Harrison's knee and the other standing in front of the whole group. He didn't want me to miss out on a chance like this. I still love that picture and the memories it evokes. I have had it framed and it hangs in my study at home. It is one of my proudest possessions.

I remember other trips with my parents. We went to America once; because of my mother's fear of flying, my father reluctantly agreed to go by boat. It took four days there and four days back and we were all terribly seasick. I don't think he ever forgave her. We went out on the *Queen Elizabeth* and came back on the *Queen Mary*. I was particularly impressed by the glitzy evenings. My mother always went down to dinner in the most glamorous dresses – one, I remember, was golden yellow with beads around the neck. Her hair was back-combed in the typical 1960s style and she looked absolutely stunning. I must have been about six and I can recall it as if it were yesterday.

My father had obviously made his mark in business by then, but I did not think of him as wealthy. If I thought about it at all, I suppose I just accepted that he was comfortably off. Nothing about the way we lived made me think any differently. He didn't drive a Rolls-Royce and our house was no bigger than my schoolfriends' houses. I didn't go to private school, initially; I attended Biggin Hill Primary School until I was nine and nothing special was made of me there; quite the opposite, in fact.

I was terribly introverted at school, particularly with the male teachers and the headmaster, Mr Huckle, who used to scare me terribly. I seemed to hate all the men teachers, and in the end the headmaster recommended that I be moved to an all-girls' school, which was probably the most sensible suggestion he ever made. I was just more comfortable with women. I asked my mother about that later and she said she thought it might have been because I was frightened at a young age by my Uncle Terry, who was a disciplinarian.

I don't remember having a friend in the world at primary school. I faked illness to avoid school, I hated it so much. I was extremely shy right through my teens; I don't know why, I just was. I think, maybe, it had to do with my mother's over-protectiveness. I felt isolated and I also felt too shy even to tell them how isolated and unhappy I was.

Dinner times were my worst nightmare. I hated eating anyway, and I am still very picky about my food. There was an awful dinner lady called Mrs Saunders, who tried to make me eat my vegetables, but I would button my lips so tight she virtually had to force-feed me. The only saving grace was a lovely dinner lady called Dorothy, who had a Cockney accent. I think she felt sorry for me and did what she could to build me up. I remember that I only liked puddings and absolutely hated vegetables, but you couldn't have your pudding until you had eaten all your vegetables, so I used to keep one Brussels sprout in my cheek, eat my pudding, and then spit the sprout out. I hated Brussels sprouts most of all; I still do.

Dorothy is now one of my closest friends. By the strangest of coincidences, Tony, the man I married, was her son. I was always very fond of her I and remember her very clearly from my school days. I lost contact with her for years, but fate brought us together again in later life.

I was a real ugly duckling. I think I was picked on by other children because I was very small and looked a lot younger than I was. I was the only one who wore glasses – I hated my National Health Service pair and often left them off. Mr Huckle drew a pair of spectacles on the bookcase in front of my desk to remind me to wear them; if he caught me without them, he made me wear his half-moon spectacles, which was very embarrassing. Not only did I wear glasses; I had an eye patch over one lens to strengthen my weaker eye, which made me clumsier and even more self-conscious. We used to play kiss-chase, but no one ever chased me.

I had very long hair pulled back tight into a pony tail which the other children used to pull. My mother would never allow me to wear my hair loose, although I tried to draw my hair over my face because I was very conscious of my high forehead and my widow's peak, or cow's lick. I desperately wanted a fringe to hide it and begged my mother to let me have one. In the end, when I was about nine years old, she agreed and took me to a hairdresser's in Beckenham. When I sat down in the chair, full of excitement, the hairdresser told my mother that a fringe was impossible because of my hairline. I was devastated. But my mother agreed; I had had a fringe when I was about five and it just used to split in two. I left without one.

Outside school my cousins, Stephanie and Russell, were my closest friends; I never had the opportunity to make friends of my own. They used to come to dinner every Wednesday with my Auntie Heather and Uncle Terry and that would be the highlight of my week. The children would be put to bed in my parents' bedroom, next to mine, while the grown-ups ate downstairs. But, of course, we never slept – it was all too exciting, and this was our time to play. I still remember with affection how soft my dad was with us: we could get away with murder. Terry, however, was the opposite.

My mother, I remember, had millions of pairs of shoes and every Wednesday night, religiously, we used to sit by our bedroom doors having shoe fights, hurling them backwards and forwards between the two rooms and squealing with delight. My father would come to the bottom of the stairs and say very quietly: 'Be quiet now, girls,' and we would wait a minute until he had gone, and then start again in a new frenzy, knowing that any minute Terry would come up and really smack my cousins.

Vanessa was very young at this stage, and she and I never really hit it off as children. There was a big age gap anyway, and as she grew older and became lonelier she wanted to be with me all the time. But when I needed a friend, she was too young to be of any assistance. She was only two years old when I was nine and started at Baston School, which was in Hayes, Bromley, Kent. This was the private girls' school of the area and I was always being told how much it cost my parents to send me there. I had to start in the middle of a school year and it was all very daunting and strange. Although I was glad to get away from Mr Huckle, I now had a new headmistress, Mrs Wimble, who was also terrifying. I called her the woman with the wobbly head, because it always seemed to be nodding.

My uniform was brown and gold, and we had to wear capes and berets in winter and blazers and boaters in summer. The children from Hayes Comprehensive used to tease me rotten when I stepped off the school bus: they called me a 'Baston Bogey'. Those first few years at Baston coincided with the most difficult years of my life, the time when my parents eventually split up. I was twelve years old.

Looking back now, I think that my parents were never really suited. I don't remember many rows, but there was always a lot of tension.

Dad was often away from home and my mother seemed very edgy. When they split up I was devastated. My schooling was affected and I had to stay down a year. I have never felt so lonely in all my life. What made matters worse was that within a few months of my father leaving, my mother's boyfriend, John, moved in. I don't remember my parents ever sitting down with me and explaining the situation; it just happened. It seemed that they had been drifting apart for years and had both, simultaneously, found other partners.

I loved my dad very much and had a very high respect for him because he was always so kind and warm. I felt then, and for a long time afterwards, that I didn't really know him and I deeply regret that we weren't closer when I was young, partly because he was so busy and partly because of the circumstances. After he left home he religiously came to see Vanessa and me every Thursday night, right up until I left home. He would just sit there and try to talk to us; often we would be more interested in watching television. It must have been very difficult for him: John was living in the family house and used to disappear for those two hours when my father was there.

However, Dad used to take us out occasionally, and we would have a fabulous time; I felt freer than I ever did at home. Mum only let him take us out every now and again and when he did there would be strict instructions about not driving at more than 30 m.p.h. (40 on the motorway!), so it was often more trouble than it was worth for him.

It was an unhappy and difficult time for me, not just because my father had left but because this stranger had come into our home. John is nine years younger than my mother and has no children of his own. He worked in computers at a London college and all I remember about him at that time – apart from resenting him terribly, because he wasn't Dad – was that he was a hard task-master. He and I used to have dreadful rows and I was terribly unhappy. I think I suffered more than Vanessa because I was a bit older. She was too young to pick up the vibes. One night I was so upset, I climbed out of my bedroom window and ran away. I wanted to go and live with my father at his flat in Croydon. It was the middle of the night and I was picked up by the police, who didn't believe my story about walking home from a party and made me get in their patrol car. They took me to my father's flat and he was very shocked to see me – mainly because he was going on a skiing holiday at 7 a.m. the next day and the friends who were going with him were staying the night.

I think he felt very guilty about it, but he drove me home and watched as I climbed back in through my bedroom window. We'd had a long chat and he had made me feel better and promised to come and see me as soon as his holiday was over. I thought that I had escaped detection, but about a week later I realized that John must have found out, because I came home one day and found him nailing up my bedroom window.

My attitude toward John was: 'Who does he think he is, telling me what to do?' People occasionally introduced him as my step-father and I was indignant and told them that I already had a father. Later, he and my mother split up for a few years: he left her for someone else. This was partly due to our constant rowing because I was so hostile to him, and I think he and Mum had rows because of me. However, they got back together and were married in 1989.

My mother and I are very close now and I love her dearly, but our relationship deteriorated during that period and I think we both wish that we had understood each other better. However, she is a gentle and caring person and I have no doubt whatsoever that she has always loved me and tried to do her best for me. What daughter can ask for more than that?

My relationship with Penny, the woman my father moved in with, was also strained. She worked at the office and was a first-rate secretary, but to me she appeared very unemotional. At the time I felt she resented me, although now I realize she just didn't know how to handle the situation. My father and Penny are still together

twenty years on and we get on fine now. She is very good for my dad
and they have made a success of their life together.

It was probably partly because of all the pain and confusion I
was feeling at this time in my life that I started to take an interest
in puzzles. Looking back, I realize it was a way of escaping from it
all. I had always wanted to work – there was something about
working and earning money that motivated me. My mother says I
inherited that from my dad. It was certainly Dad who offered me
money to design puzzles for his crossword magazines. He gave me
50p a puzzle. I have always loved doing anything with words: I still
love crosswords and puzzles and I am a demon Scrabble-player,
and I made up puzzles in my spare time to earn a little extra cash. I
used to sell them in batches of 100. Goodness knows what the
people doing the puzzles would have thought if they knew they were
being designed by a thirteen-year-old. I took it very seriously and
even visited libraries to research a subject. 'Find a Word', where you
had to make a number of words out of one word or subject, was my
speciality. I would spend hours poring over my puzzles and working
out how much I could make, motivated by the lure of the 50p piece.

It was also around this time that I started to make friends at
school. All of a sudden I seemed to fit in better with the girls in my
class. There were three in particular: Stephanie 'Stevie' Lyons,
Karen Carter and Beverley Dalton. Stevie was a bridesmaid at my
wedding, but now lives abroad, Karen and I drooled over Donny
Osmond and David Cassidy, and Beverley was the bad influence.
She was really an awakening for me. She was very street-wise for
her age and I was very naive because I had been so sheltered. I
learned about sex at school, first from friends and then from
biology lessons. I remember thinking how cold and clinical it all
seemed and I was pleased to discover later that the reality was a lot
better!

Beverley wore make-up and I looked up to her. I had no dress
sense at all and was still very unattractive – freckly, pasty and very
skinny – which didn't help my confidence. It was only when I

reached the age of seventeen that I started to blossom, and after that I always had a very curvaceous figure. But at that time the boys were always interested in Beverley, not me, although through her I came to meet boys and it was like Christmas.

I could have done a lot better at school because I was intelligent, but I didn't because I was not dedicated enough. I ended up with O-levels in Art, Needlework, English Lang, Cookery (I was quite good), History, French, Maths and Biology. Nothing there to suggest a budding businesswoman, and my mother will tell you that I only passed many of those exams by staying up revising the night before and learning huge chunks of data parrot-fashion.

By the time my education was important I was more interested in boys and money than my classes. I even worked on the puzzles during my lessons, and put far more effort and energy into working during the holidays than I ever did at school, because I wanted to earn money: it was a big incentive.

Chapter Two
SEX AND THE WORKING GIRL

MY SISTER AND I used to go to dancing lessons at the Shirley Cox School. We learned Latin American and ballroom dancing, all of which I have now completely forgotten. Shirley Cox's son was a dancer there and he was brilliant. His name was Spencer Harradine and he was two years older than me. He was not particularly attractive, because he wore spectacles and had moles, but he was a great dancer. I was about fifteen and I was very impressed. All the girls had been out with him and I wanted to go out with him too. In the event I was invited round to his house but I was so nervous that I pinned the top of my jeans together with a safety pin to stop him from going too far. It worked, up to a point, but I remember that we kissed very clumsily and caressed each other on the bathroom floor. Going out with Spencer was more a matter of prestige than anything, and after being thoroughly mauled I decided he was very unattractive and wondered what all the fuss had been about. It had been my first kiss.

Later, after I left school, I met my first teenage love, Graham Vale. He was the brother of Pauline, a girl who worked at the Beauty Box beauty parlour in Biggin Hill, where I had a part-time job. It was all blue rinses and old ladies and I had to wash hair and sweep the floors. I hated it. The woman who ran it was very bossy. She knew my dad, which is probably the only reason I lasted so long. I left before I could be fired.

I thought Pauline Vale was really *it*, and when her brother came to pick her up after work one day, I was smitten; I thought he was absolutely gorgeous – 6 foot 2 inches tall, with blond hair and bright blue eyes. He was a lathe operator at the local airfield and his father was in property. I was sixteen and in love. Pauline told him I fancied him and set up a date with him at the flying club, which my father owned. We met at the disco there and went out together for ten months. I thought I was madly in love with him, but looking back I must have been the most boring girl to be with. I had zero personality and zero confidence, and not a lot happened in that ten months. We didn't even have sex.

My relationship with Graham was doomed. He dumped me for an older woman and I was devastated. I remember it vividly: he drove me home one night from Tatsfield Working Men's Club; as we sat in the car, he said, 'It's over, I've met someone else.' He then proceeded to tell me all about her – she was older and had lovely long hair (mine was shoulder length) – to really rub salt into the wound.

My mother was furious with him for upsetting me. She even made me give his Christmas present back – a bottle of Tramp perfume! I continued to go round to the club to see him for a while, but he was always there with his new girlfriend, so I forced myself to move on to pastures new. It felt like months before I was over it. He was the only man ever to dump me and I decided there and then that I never wanted to feel that bad again.

After the Beauty Box I went on to work as a waitress at the Spinning Wheel restaurant at Westerham, where I was not a great success either. Then I worked briefly at the Surrey & Kent Flying Club at Biggin Hill, making sandwiches behind the bar. The aerodrome was much busier in those days and the club was always full.

For a while I decided I wanted to be a window dresser: I am quite creative and I liked painting at school and the idea really appealed to me, but I was torn because I also wanted to work for myself. I was inspired by things I read about successful people and, although I didn't know exactly *what* I wanted to do, I did know that I had to make something of my life. I used to come up with all these different ideas, like running a sandwich van — nothing too ambitious. I was always very structured and organized and quite analytical in my thinking. I had plans and was always on the go. But what probably inspired me at the beginning was the idea of becoming independent, both personally and financially. I felt trapped by the situation at home and I wanted to break away.

My dad knew I was really down in the dumps over Graham, so he set me up on a blind date with a young man called Martin Thomas at the Biggin Hill Flying Club dinner dance. Martin looked like John Travolta and I thought he was wonderful. It was lust at first sight (I have met him since at a restaurant in Covent Garden: he came over to my table to say hello, and I didn't recognize him — he looks more like Bruce Willis now!).

Martin was a petrol pump attendant, and after the dinner dance I started to see him regularly and used to stay at his house in the valley of Biggin Hill. My mother objected very strongly to him. One night, when I was about seventeen, I was walking home from the airfield and my mum and my grandmother and Vanessa came screeching up in Mum's car and she started screaming at me. My grandmother had found some condoms which I had hidden in my room and had told my mum. She was furious. It was mortifying to be told off there and then in the middle of the street. When she was finished, she drove off again at high speed and I was left to walk home, shame-faced. I was always very unlucky at being caught.

As you will have gathered from that last story, Martin was the first boyfriend I slept with. I felt I had been waiting a long time; it was good to start experimenting, and experiment we did! Martin must have enjoyed it anyway, because he presented me with a diamond and sapphire engagement ring about eighteen months later. It just seemed a natural progression. I don't know why, I didn't think about the marriage part; I just saw us getting engaged and having a big party, which we did at the Biggin Hill Flying Club.

By then my mother had calmed down a bit about Martin and didn't mind as long as I was safe and happy. My dad, however, was always trying to talk me out of it. Even though he had set me up with Martin, he didn't want me to marry him; he thought I was going to turn out like a lot of young girls, who married too young and had five kids. He kept telling me, 'You are too young, live your life.' But the more he went on at me, the more determined I became.

The crazy thing was that Martin and I rowed all the time, but we always assumed we would stay together. We never set the wedding date, which is just as well, because I ended up breaking off the engagement a few months later after I met someone else, a guy called Andy Hawkins. We had a fling while I was still with Martin, which Martin never knew about (until now!). Andy and I met at a party after Martin and I had another row and he had stormed off home. Andy was very nice and he really did want a proper relationship, but I realized later that the only reason I went out with him was because he looked like Graham – whom I still often thought about.

Then, while I was still seeing Andy and Martin, I met Tony D'Silva. It was after yet another row with Martin that I went over to the Sport Air Club and started talking to this dark, handsome stranger. I realized almost immediately that I really liked him . . . OK, I thought he was fantastic, actually. He was quite different from anyone I had ever met – Anglo-Indian, with black hair and an attractive face. He had a Mark 4 Cortina and his own house. He was a diamond sorter for De Beers. Having gone from a lathe operator to a petrol pump attendant, this guy was the one for me.

I went straight back home after meeting Tony, and proceeded to dump Andy and Martin – Andy on the telephone immediately and Martin a few weeks later. After we had had a row, I would usually ring Martin and make the peace. This time I didn't, and he held out for two weeks before calling me. By then I was seeing Tony regularly and I told Martin I had met someone else. I think he must have been shocked, although he was probably relieved too because he didn't protest. As for the engagement ring, I seem to remember I had already flung it back at him during one of our fights.

Shortly after I met Tony I went to work for Royal Doulton at Medhursts department store in Bromley (now called Allders). I walked in one day and asked the manageress for a Saturday job. My mum and my grandmother threw their hands up in horror when I told them, knowing how clumsy I was.

My boss was a lady called Coral Boyce; she was very amusing and left in the end to pursue her hobby: acting. In one of the many coincidences in my life, quite recently Vanessa and I were watching *Noel's House Party* on television together and Vanessa said, 'Isn't that your old boss?' and there she was on my television screen – Coral Boyce, a bit-part actress in 'Gotcha!'.

I worked at Royal Doulton first on Saturdays and then during the school holidays and then full-time after I left school. I had to wear a white shirt and a navy skirt, and a badge. It was extremely quiet; the arrival of a customer was a major event. I wanted to be rushed off my feet but that only happened during the sales. The best times were when my friend Stevie Lyons came to work there but she didn't stay long.

Soon after that I was offered a trainee manager's position, but I decided not to take it. The job just wasn't stimulating enough. I didn't know what I wanted to do, so I spoke to my father. I remember standing in the lounge at my mother's house and telling him that I needed a full-time job. I didn't have anything particular in mind, but I told him that I wanted to work at the firm, which was then called Gold Star. He said, 'Yes,' but I could see in his face that he was thinking, 'Oh no!' I could tell. I think he still thought that I would just get married and have kids. I can understand why he might have thought that then, and I suppose my working for him was just another thing to worry about.

When I started at Gold Star in January 1979 I was still living at home with my mother in Biggin Hill, and each morning I was collected for work by one of my father's board members, David Tizzard, who lived near by. Poor man, he was my boss and had the job of looking after me. Initially I worked on the computer, entering the wholesale and export figures. I was paid £45 a week. Later, when I moved into wages, I discovered that the tea lady earned more than me and I was very depressed.

There were probably about ninety people working at Gold Star then, a quarter of the staff employed now, and I didn't know any of them. Because I had done a bit of typing at school I picked up the computer very quickly and was put somewhere where I couldn't do any harm. It was awful; I hated it. My relationship with my father was very difficult: we didn't really know each other and I only saw him about once a week. I just didn't feel wanted there. I knew that he didn't think the job was going to be anything more than a stop-gap for me, especially after I had started going out with Tony. There was generally a very unpleasant atmosphere – not only between us, but throughout the company. There was no team spirit and I don't think that had anything to do with the product; it was just the way things were being run. Matters were made worse when, soon after I joined, the girlfriend or wife of the Export Manager also started work there. She was employed as a temp and she really intimidated me. She was openly abrasive towards me, and I can only assume it was because I was the boss's daughter. I don't remember anyone else treating me like that. They would certainly never have been given any reason to feel threatened because I was so timid.

This girl and I were working side by side and she was very quick on the computer. The only good that came out of the situation was that I improved my typing skills enormously because of the competition I was up against. I complained about her a couple of times, but it didn't get me anywhere and she continued to make my life miserable – I even thought about leaving. It definitely damaged my relationship with her husband, which was to play a part in the future. Thankfully, I was transferred to the Accounts Department after a while, which was a great relief. I think I was just being moved around to different areas to see where I worked best.

But I was out of the frying pan and into the fire, because the accountant at that time seemed to spend the whole time breathing down my cleavage (and he had incredibly bad breath).

My salary rose fractionally each year with the annual increments, but I was still paid very badly. I would think about leaving and talk to Tony about it, and he would tell me to talk to my father first. When I did, nothing ever came of it because my father had this clever way of persuading you that everything was all right. He is very calming and gives you a false sense of security. I always felt much better when I left him, even though there was still that distance between us. Dad was always very accessible to all his employees. He was one of those bosses who would sometimes be behind a desk in his office and sometimes working the fork-lift truck on the shop floor. He was, and is, very hands-on. If I wanted to speak to him I had to try and catch him in his office for five minutes. My uncle was on a different floor and I didn't see him at all; we were never particularly close. Once again, I felt very isolated.

The late seventies and early eighties were interesting times at Gold Star because we were raided by the police every eighteen months or so in their big crackdowns on so-called obscenity. I probably experienced two or three raids during my early days there. These were very depressing, not only for me but for all the staff; it was a time of low morale for everyone. You would arrive for work one morning and the police would be waiting – about fifteen of them in plain clothes.

When you read all the publicity about the raids at the time, the impression given is of fast action, high drama, with lorry-loads of girlie mags being snatched from under our noses. In truth it was all done very quickly and quietly, like a well-rehearsed play, and they would confiscate just about everything – the majority of the publications taken were 'normal' women's magazines and books that would be considered tame by anybody's standards. Our warehouse staff would always co-operate and help load the magazines into the lorries, which normally took a whole day. It wasn't for the officers there to decide what was obscene or not; the law stated that they had to take the lot and let others decide. The police officers were from what was known then as the Porn Squad, and it all seemed to be just a matter of form because nothing ever came of it. The magazines were very often returned a year or so later, without a prosecution having been made. By then they were out of date and although we could sell some to the American market, the rest had to be scrapped. It all cost the business a lot of money.

They always raided the business premises – ours at Whyteleafe, the distribution centre at Eagle Wharf Road, Islington, North London, and the wholesalers and the printers – but never the homes of the people running the company. My father rarely dealt with them personally; the warehouse staff and those directors who came in early made sure the police had what they needed.

The adult magazine side of the business didn't bother me and I have never tried to hide it from anyone. My attitude has always been: if you want it, buy it, and if you don't, then don't. When I was young, if anyone asked me what my father did I just said he was a publisher. I never made a conscious effort to hide what he published from anyone; it was just an accurate description of his job. There were never girlie magazines lying around the house or anything like that; Dad was a very professional person. I think people assume that because someone sells magazines like that, he must somehow be different.

I do remember odd comments made by the milkman and the cleaner which, when I look back now, fit into the jigsaw. My mother was worried about things we might hear because by then my father was quite well known. It was only when I started working at Gold Star that I fully realized what some of the products were. As a child, if I ever found anything at home it was only because I had been delving where I shouldn't. I once stole a book I found in my father's briefcase and smuggled it into school. I showed it to the girls behind the pavilion and, after the initial shock, they thought I was great; for a while I had a following of girls who wanted to see it.

There were a number of controversial court cases my father and uncle were involved in at that time; I didn't know anything about them until I was grown up. I look back now and read the cuttings and wonder how it could have been kept from me. I also wonder, incidentally, how a lot of the cases even came to be brought to court. The rules on what was or was not obscene or likely to deprave in the sixties and seventies were very different to what they are today and, indeed, all the majority of juries acquitted my father and Ralph on all charges, much to the consternation of people like Mary Whitehouse.

In the most celebrated case in 1964 (when I was four), Ralph appeared at Bow Street Magistrates Court after police seized almost 200 copies of the eighteenth-century sex novel *Fanny Hill: Memoirs of a Coxcomb*, written by John Cleland in 1749. The court asked Ralph why the books should not be destroyed, and Mayflower Books got historians and authors to give evidence on his behalf, including one who claimed that the book was actually quite revolutionary for its era because it marked a first step in the emancipation of women by telling the story from Fanny's viewpoint and detailing her obvious enjoyment of sex. Sadly, they lost the case, which seems incredible now that the book is openly sold in bookshops.

Eight years later Dad and Ralph appeared voluntarily before Lord Longford's commission on pornography, only to be described by him as 'leaders of the pornographic book trade in Britain'. He did, however, add that some of the articles they published in their magazines were informative and instructive and should be available on the National Health Service!

One of the cuttings at the time quotes Dad as saying: 'You won't find any hard porn in our shops. There are no back rooms. Everything is on view at the front of the shop. We draw the line at pornography. The difficulty is that the line keeps moving and a publication which is acceptable today might not be acceptable tomorrow.' He added that what he was hoping for from Lord

Longford's commission was guidance on where to draw the line. I have always considered him ahead of his time in the sexual revolution: he once told journalists: 'We have always presented sex in a healthy and positive light, and we feel that both men and women should be given the freedom of choice to buy products that enhance their sex lives.' This really sums up how we, as a family, feel about the sex industry.

My only criticism of the business was that it was a bit one-sided; I would have felt more comfortable if there had been products for women as well. I am comfortable with anything as long as it is balanced, but this business has always been geared towards men. I first visited the sex shops with Tony when I was a young woman. Even though they were the best in Soho, they were very seedy. There were film booths where people could sit and watch short erotic films. The managers said the worst moments were when the film jammed and all these red-faced men would come out of the booths to complain! It certainly didn't turn me on and I wouldn't have gone into the shops on my own; it was not so much the product as the environment.

I am always surprised when I hear how the public view those who work in the Gold group of companies. They are just like those in any other company — a cross-section of people working in a factory and offices in the suburbs of London; we could just as well be selling baked beans. The staff are happy to have a job in a secure industry. There is a bus stop outside the head office at Whyteleafe and you still see people staring in, waiting for something illegal or immoral to happen. It's hilarious.

It is also amusing to watch the reactions of people who come in from the outside, like telephone engineers or workmen. You can see them constantly looking over their shoulder as if waiting for the nude woman in the PVC coat to walk through the office in front of them. I once took a cab to Gold Star and the driver said to me, 'You're not going in there, are you, luv? You know what goes on in there!' I said: 'No, tell me!' but he didn't have an answer.

Well aware of this attitude, in those early days if anyone asked me what I did I told them I worked for a publishing company. I didn't encourage people to read anything into it; my job as an office junior wasn't anything to be proud of anyway. I just felt I was biding my time until something happened.

That something did happen when I did a stint on the mail order. The environment there was much nicer: there were more people and it had a friendlier atmosphere. I was administering the contact ads, which is like the personal ads in the back of the magazines. People wrote in with their photographs and said what sort of partner or relationship they were looking for, and the person placing the ad would leave a box number and we would send the details on. We had to make them sign disclaimers that said they were seeking partners for pleasure, not profit, in an attempt to weed out prostitutes, although few prostitutes could have afforded to advertise regularly. It was all run by one lady from the editorial department. She worked alongside the people doing the puzzles, so I helped out briefly.

At that time the Gold Group comprised Gold Star, in publishing, and Ann Summers, which was then just sex shops and mail order, and a couple of distribution companies. We were fairly small. We didn't have our own printers then, just a few depots around the country. The Ann Summers mail order system was located near our offices, and that is how I came to stumble across the next stage of my career.

There was a very nice, bubbly lady called Marlene Green in mail order, who was dealing single-handedly with all the Ann Summers orders. Her life started to get complicated when Chris Rogers and Ann Galea came in and asked if they could buy some goods on a wholesale basis. They said they were working for the Pippa Dee party plan company, and had been into the Ann Summers shops and thought it would be a great idea to sell some of our goods along with the Pippa Dee range.

The company agreed to supply them on a wholesale basis. It

made good business sense: the women collected the goods themselves, probably about £100 worth a time, and loaded up their car.
Marlene moaned about them because it was all extra work for her,
but I was impressed by their enthusiasm. After overhearing their
conversations, I began to understand the idea behind the concept.
I started chatting to them and asked if I could come to one of their
parties. It was early 1981 and I had been working for my father for
two years, and that is how I came to be at the Thamesmead party
attempting to draw Tony's meat and two veg.

When I was invited to that party, Tony and I had been married for
less than a year. He really was my first true love. We didn't argue,
like I had with Martin, and I was very proud to have him because he
was a prime catch. He took me to meet his parents fairly soon after
we met, although not immediately. Until we met up again Dorothy
and I never realized that we knew each other from years before. She
recognized me straight away and I was amazed to see my kindly
dinner lady from Biggin Hill Primary School. It was so strange
meeting her in those circumstances. We were both stunned. I think
I was a little embarrassed because of Tony and I didn't want to
discuss my difficult childhood and the dreadful school mealtimes
there and then, although much later we did talk about all of that
and had a good laugh.

I also met Tony's father, Derek, who looks like Omar Sharif and
is extremely charming – a real gentleman. We hit it off really well.

I moved into Tony's little two-up, two-down in Rochester
within six months of meeting him. I was nineteen. My dad was fine
about me leaving home, and my mum was all right until the
moment I moved my things out to pack into Tony's car. Just as I was
about to go she became a bit irrational, which is not unusual for a
mother at such a time.

Vanessa, aged twelve, was still at home and I didn't register then
how upset *she* was about me leaving, but she told me later that the
moment I closed the door she burst into tears because she realized

that she was now truly alone. I didn't understand how she felt until several years later.

I was very excited about moving in with Tony. I had been collecting for my bottom drawer for years, mainly a superb range of Royal Doulton china. His house was equipped with furniture from a house clearance his mum had heard about – all old bits and pieces I didn't want in my home. We decided to bundle it all up and sell the lot at Rochester Market. I marked all the goods at 50p or £1 each and we sold everything. It went so well that we took a stall for a few more weeks and went round to my parents' and Tony's parents' and persuaded them to give us all their unwanted bric-à-brac to sell. That was my first experience of direct selling and I loved it.

As soon as I moved in and had all my things around me, I wanted to get organized. I went round the house tidying it up all the time and made it very homely. I think I even made curtains. That was when I discovered that Tony was the most untidy man I have ever met: he would even leave drawers and cupboard doors open. He once defrosted the entire contents of the fridge because he didn't shut the door. Initially, I wanted to do all the things associated with running a home. Many women will, I am sure, identify with what I went through – you make the house beautiful and cook lovely dinners, so that your partner can say you are wonderful, and when he asks if he can help you make the fatal mistake of saying no, and a couple of months pass and you are left wondering when he is ever going to offer to help again and, of course, he never does.

We were soon into quite a routine: we would go off to work each morning, him catching his train to London and me catching mine. Then I started taking driving lessons, and finally passed my test at the third attempt. I bought myself a car (a Mustard-coloured Mini bought in instalments from Uncle Ralph's wife, Annie), so I had some independence – which was just as well, because a few months after I moved in Tony was transferred to Antwerp for six months. I stayed on in the house in Rochester on my own and travelled over to see him for the weekend once a month. Because I was still a teenager I could get a special rate ferry ticket, although it was quite a trek. I used to go up to London, catch a train to Folkestone, take the ferry to Ostend, change at Ghent and go on to Antwerp. I was a young girl travelling alone, often in the middle of the night; Tony, as far as I remember, came home for the weekend only once in all that time.

With Tony in Antwerp and me at Gold Star I was feeling pretty frustrated and hard done by. I was really struggling to make ends meet, especially with the journeys back and forth to Belgium. I had lost touch with a few friends because of my relationship with Tony and I didn't seem to have very much to look forward to. Then Tony came back from Antwerp and we started to talk about getting married. I was still only nineteen.

It was great to have something else to focus my mind on. We set the date – first in January, then June, and finally 20 August 1980. I was really looking forward to it; I never had any nerves and was in my element organizing it all. I worked in the office nine-to-five, Monday to Friday, and although I have never envisaged being broody or being tied down with kids, I did want to be married and have a nice house and husband.

I was also set on the full white wedding. Tony was Catholic and so we had to have a Catholic ceremony, although we had a sort of semi-service and were spared the full-length one, because my mother was Church of England and my father was half-Jewish. It took place in a grotty little church in Haig Road, Biggin Hill, but the lady who lived opposite very kindly allowed us to go into her garden, which was full of roses, for the photographs. It was a glorious day and everything went wonderfully. I remember my mouth ached terribly the next day from smiling so much.

My mother helped me with the arrangements, and my father paid for it all. The reception cost about £1,600 and my dress came from Pronuptia and seemed very expensive at the time. About 200 people came to the reception at the Grasshopper restaurant in

Westerham; I had invited everyone I knew. I had three bridesmaids. Vanessa was thirteen and still a real tomboy – another little ugly duckling (she is really beautiful now) – and she hated me for months afterwards for making her wear a pretty blue floral dress. The other bridesmaids were my cousin Stephanie and my friend Stevie, both aged twenty-one. We drove off from the wedding in a white Rolls-Royce. Tony wore a beige suit, not top hat and tails, and, in my opinion, looked gorgeous.

After such a lovely wedding, our honeymoon was disastrous. My husband, I had come to realize, was just a little bit mean when it came to money. He splashed out on everyone else but cut the corners at home. He had made a lot of money in Antwerp, but instead of paying for a nice honeymoon, he bought himself a second-hand cabin cruiser and a souped-up Mini. (We went down the Medway once with the cabin cruiser and it was a complete disaster: we were just not cut out for boating – it was too much like hard work; the second time we took it out the motor went.) Originally we were going to honeymoon in the cabin cruiser, but it wasn't ready in time so Tony announced we were going to France instead, which sounded great.

Everything started well: my father flew us to Perpignan, where we met up with a friend of Tony's and his girlfriend who had a tent in the South of France. That is when things started to go badly wrong. I argued with this girl the whole time we were there and I also suffered very bad sunstroke. The four of us slept in this tent and it was dreadful – not my idea of a romantic honeymoon at all.

When we returned home and settled into married life, we moved house, selling Tony's place in Rochester and buying a three-bedroom semi in King's Road, Biggin Hill, which needed masses of work doing on it. Tony, I discovered, was excellent at supervising, but as I was very keen to get on with it, I did all the wallpapering and DIY while he looked on. He would rope his parents in whenever there was some really hard work to do. It was not a particularly old house, but I loved it. Even though we argued a bit about the mess and him not getting on and doing things, in those first few years we were generally very happy; but I was now ready to move forward in my career.

Chapter Three
BLOOD, SWEAT AND TEARS

THE PARTY AT THAMESMEAD was really the cata-lyst for everything. After the buzz I got from that, it was hard to think straight. But I knew I had to stop and consider very carefully before I made the next move: no one was going to share my enthusiasm until they knew what I was talking about. I realized that I really needed to do a bit more homework. I wasn't going to reveal my secret plan until I had researched it more thoroughly.

At home, I spoke to Tony, and between us we decided to hold some parties ourselves. I didn't want to join Pippa Dee; I just wanted to test the idea. We knew from our experiences at Rochester Market that direct selling could be lucrative, and we worked out a plan of action, which included ploughing all our spare cash into some stock. We drove up to the Mile End Road and Commercial Road in the East End of London and persuaded the shops to sell items of clothing to us, even though we weren't in business yet. They had a policy of selling a minimum of one hundred items, but we didn't want that many, so we said we would like a few samples first to see how they would sell. Somehow we convinced them and we walked off with ten of each item. Tony was a very good nego-tiator and he liked going in and haggling with them. We bought jumpers, skirts, dresses and jackets – I think we invested about £100. I picked up an old clothes rail from the back of Debenhams in Bromley after sweet-talking a man in overalls.

To start with I had parties at our house, and then I sold to people on an individual basis at the airfield or persuaded others to let me hold parties at their homes. My first proper party was at the home of Sue Craddock, who happened to live opposite my old boyfriend, Martin, and I remember his sister and mother turning up as well. My most popular lines were jumpers with appliqué on and some bomber jackets which were very lightweight and came in pastel shades of pink and lemon. I remember seeing a girl wearing one in Biggin Hill and I was very excited to see one of my jackets on the street.

At these parties I did just what I had seen the demonstrator from Pippa Dee do. It was strange – I was still quite shy, but somehow I managed to stand up with my goods and sell them to people. I think it was because I was so passionate about the idea behind it. I demonstrated the clothes, holding them up and telling people about them, and then invited my guests to the rail to pick what they wanted. For the next party I prepared a big spread of food at home, having invited family and friends. Funnily enough, Andy Hawkins's mother turned up at that one and kept asking me: 'Don't I know you from somewhere?' I just pretended not to recognize her.

Tony and I had a weekly routine: we would drive to London to buy the goods each Sunday and sell them through the week. By this time I had exchanged my Mini for a silver Ford Fiesta and we used to pack it to the brim and come home again to unload and price everything up ready for the next sale. We were getting quite a good return – after all, we had no overheads – but we couldn't have made a living from it. The idea was to reinvest in the stock. It was all part of my grand plan.

I did very well at the parties I held. What I wasn't so good at (like many of the new recruits to party plan) was persuading other people to hold parties. I think I was carried away by the sales side, but if your business is to grow it needs to keep branching out into different areas. I think I probably only held about six parties in all over two or three months before it started to peter out. But at about the same time, Marlene was complaining anew about the paperwork Chris and Ann were creating for her, so I decided then that the time was right for my big move.

I knew that this step was going to be the hardest: I would have to go and ask my father for help, but our relationship at the time was so distant that I didn't know how to approach him. I delayed for several days – there were very few opportunities to see him alone anyway. Then one night I stayed late when he was in the office he shared with David Tizzard. David didn't leave, so I just had to go in there and speak to my father in front of him. Because I was so nervous, everything came out in a rush. I made a complete botch of it. I said something like: Marlene is not happy with what she is doing, and I would like to take over the running of those accounts. I said I really wanted to take it away from her and do it myself. And then I just blurted out my idea. I rambled on about the party I had been to, and about all the women who had enjoyed themselves, and how we could set up our own Party Plan. I said he knew the sales on the wholesale side were doing well, and women wanted to buy these things, and they liked to buy them in the privacy of their own homes . . . so it was a good idea.

Dad was sitting down to start with, but he stood up halfway through my speech and just looked at me blankly when I had finished. He tells me now that it was actually a very special moment for him; it was then that he first realized that I had the makings of a businesswoman, and he was so stunned he didn't want to say or do anything to burst the bubble. When he had regained his composure he told me, in very measured tones, that he was happy for me to take over the administrative side but, as for the parties, we would have to hold a meeting and I would have to present my idea to the board. He was basically saying, Go away and think about it. I felt he knew I had made a hash of it and was giving me a second chance.

I had always been a good planner, but I didn't know how to make a presentation to the board. I guessed it would be just like doing a school report, putting things in the right order and setting it all out, so I sat down and thought about all the things spinning round in my head. I started that evening and wrote it out by hand a dozen times before neatly typing it up. I recited it to Tony several times and he said it sounded all right.

I knew the board were already discussing problems of the wholesale side and it was on the agenda for the next meeting anyway. I had about a week to prepare myself and, when the day came, I thought I would die I was so nervous! The board then consisted of Dad, my uncle Ralph, John Gibbins, who was Managing Director of GBD (one of our subsidiaries), David Tizzard, who was Sales Manager, Ray Unadkat, Group Accountant and Ron Coleman, Director.

I waited in my office while the meeting began and became more and more nervous. I had never even spoken to John Gibbins. Ron Coleman had an abrasive manner, so he was fairly daunting. Even with David Tizzard, who used to drive me to the office, I hadn't built up any sort of relationship, and I still didn't really know my father or Ralph. To me this boardroom meeting was like going to see five Mr Huckles all at once.

The call came from my father that they were ready to see me, and I started towards the boardroom. It felt like a very long walk, down the steps and along the corridor to the end. I was shaking with the type of nervousness you feel when you really want something and you don't want to be turned down. I think I was probably more worried that they would say no than anything else. I knocked at the door and my father said, 'Come in.' They pulled up a chair for me and I sat down in front of them all. I could feel all their eyes watching me. My father said something like, 'Jacky's had an idea she wants to tell us about,' and I began.

I had two pieces of paper with me and, in a quivering little voice, I started to read from them. I had always intended just to use them as notes and ad lib the rest, but because of my lack of confidence I recited my speech religiously. I talked them through the story, labouring the point that the women I had met all thought it was a really good idea; I said we could take the product from our shop range and use the catalogues from the mail order side, so there wouldn't be much additional cost or investment. I told them how I had set up my own parties to see how the plan worked, buying my stock in London, but they didn't seem very impressed. I explained that we would recruit women as party organizers, who would sell the product range at people's homes and earn 30 per cent discount. They, too, would be encouraged to recruit their guests and host-esses as organizers, with the incentive for unit organizers of earning additional money from their recruits' sales. That way, I said, the company keeps growing and new customers are constantly introduced and new people recruited.

Ron Coleman had a habit of starting his sentences with: 'I don't care what you say,' and then dismissing your point completely. Well, at this meeting he suddenly said: 'I don't care what you say, but women aren't interested in sex.' I was staggered and even more taken aback when none of the other board members, not even my father, bothered to disagree with him.

My father was really quite hard on me. I know now that he did it because he wanted to make sure that I knew what I was doing, and that he didn't appear to be endorsing everything I said. He has always been vehemently opposed to nepotism. They cross-exam-ined me as if we were in a courtroom — my dad in particular, although at one point I did see a reassuring glance. This rather misled one or two of the board members because they just wanted to agree with whatever he said; when they started hearing negatives from him they followed his lead.

I felt very frustrated by it all because no one seemed to be on my side. David Tizzard sat on the fence. John Gibbins was actually quite positive, but he was a very positive man anyway. He knew someone who was in a Party Plan scheme, so he at least understood the principle. For about an hour I was questioned closely by all these men. Before that board meeting I think my father and every-one else thought I was just an office girl. Despite my nerves and inexperience, Dad now says, as he sat there and watched me he became quite emotional inside because he realized that maybe there was some potential here; maybe he didn't need the son he had once thought he needed to take over the business; maybe he had me instead. I think from that moment he started to look at me in a different light.

I was eventually dismissed from the board meeting and went back to my office. Of course I wanted to know what their decision was as soon as possible. No one else at Ann Summers really knew what I was up to, so I couldn't discuss it with anyone. Every time my father walked past my office, I would ask if there was any news yet. A couple of days later he summoned me and said that, provided we reiterated the terms, I was to be allowed to run the show myself using the existing facilities. They would allow me to place an advert in the *Evening Standard* once a week for a month to recruit women to be party organizers, and after they had seen what the response was they would review the position. I was over the moon!

We started off with the eight women I had met at Thamesmead who really wanted to go for it – among them Chris and Ann, the original two women. Some of them were already selling the Ann Summers products anyway at Pippa Dee parties and the others were friends and guests. Chris and Ann were the most enthusiastic – they wanted to give up Pippa Dee altogether – so they were the first to get properly started and they held the first official Ann Summers party at Thamesmead which made £83.21 in sales.

There were so many things to do. I remember thinking, 'Where do I start?' As is my way, I compiled a list. I dealt with all the invoices and calls, typing everything myself by hand, and designed a big box advert for the *Evening Standard*. I remember I had to be careful what I said. The newspaper told me I couldn't advertise for women staff only, and I had to change the word 'erotic' (as in 'erotic lingerie') to 'exotic'. In the end, I think it read something like:

DEMONSTRATORS REQUIRED TO RUN ANN SUMMERS PARTIES SELLING EXOTIC LINGERIE FOR LADIES ONLY. EARN THIRTY TO FORTY POUNDS FOR AN EVENING'S WORK. APPLY TO – [MY TELEPHONE NUMBER].

I had based the earnings on what I knew from my own parties and from the Pippa Dee women. The advert cost about £400 to place and appeared on a Wednesday in May 1981. I was inundated with phone calls. I took them all myself. A lot were from men, some asking for Ann from Ann Summers. I probably got twenty-five genuine recruits from that first ad; the rest of the calls were more curious than anything. It was so busy that I had to install an answerphone to cope.

I thought the best thing to do would be to hold seminars, so I booked a room at the Strand Palace Hotel in London for the following Thursday. I remember that the room was far too large, because when the women arrived there were a lot of empty chairs. We held a seminar every Thursday for a month, following the ads that appeared each Wednesday.

I went to the seminars with Ron Coleman, his secretary, and Chris and Ann. I would have a starter kit in the back of the car to demonstrate and several times en route I nearly turned back, I was so nervous. I made the kit up with the help of Chris and Ann, and included some of the sex aids and novelties. I was shaking so much as I stood up in front of all these women that I could feel my knees knocking together. I was still only twenty years old.

The women had this uncertain look on their faces and, as I started talking about the products, one or two of them stood up and left the room, which was really distracting. This just made me even more nervous, but I tried to concentrate my attention on those who were left. After I had finished talking I showed the women the product range, and then we walked around and spoke to them individually. Those who showed positive interest had their details logged and I made appointments to go and see them at their homes.

I designed the stationery and arranged for it to be produced at one of our printing firms – I think it cost about £2,000. When I asked for that money the board commented that they thought it was all getting a bit too expensive. They didn't really share my enthusiasm for the whole thing, although I think they realized that there was some potential there.

I was very pleased with the forty or so women we had recruited in the beginning, because they were, in turn, recruiting more people, and the whole project was expanding and self-generating. I moved into the main office where all the export was going on. I had an L-shaped desk in one corner of the room and that was the Ann Summers Party Plan office.

By this time Tony was getting more and more fed up with De Beers and was thinking of buying a local wine bar called the Hungry Toad. My father advised him against the idea and told him that if he was truly unhappy at De Beers, then he could come and work at Ann Summers too, as a junior member of staff in one of the London sex shops. Tony asked my opinion and I thought that it would be a good idea. He was much more vivacious and extrovert than I was and he did quite a good job of selling himself. Tony has always had a lot of admiration for my father, so he agreed.

Never one to be accused of nepotism, my father first put him in charge of the film booths in the Ann Summers shops we had in London – at Brewer Street, Bond Street, Wardour Street and the flagship in Charing Cross Road. It wasn't quite the lowest position in the shops – that went to the cleaner. Later, he worked at the tills and finally became Area Manager of twelve shops. I don't remember anyone being particularly horrified about his change of career from a diamond sorter to working in a chain of sex shops, but I suppose some must have been.

In those early stages I regarded the shops as entirely separate from what I was trying to do. Although Tony worked there for a while, I felt they were David and Ralph's concern. They were successful because they still attracted the dirty raincoat brigade and the tourists and the gay men. Even some of the people who worked there seemed to attract that kind of element. The gays were a big part of the customer base and the shops certainly sold a lot of the larger size nurses' uniforms and maids' outfits to the cross-dressers. They even had changing rooms for them to try on some of the outfits and Tony told me how these grown men would come out from behind the curtain dressed as schoolgirls and ask him what he thought. He couldn't tell them the truth, so he just used to say they looked very nice and leave it at that. The more outrageous items (the gags, whips, handcuffs, chains and masks) were mostly sold to impeccably dressed City gents in their pin-stripe suits – the judges, civil servants and politicians who had Eton accents and always paid in cash.

I think Tony really hoped that he was going to get on and do well in the company; he didn't want to miss out on what was happening with me. But in the end he became just as unhappy at Ann Summers because he needed constant recognition and involvement and he just felt cut off. He wanted a guarantee that he would move on and get further opportunities and that did put a strain on our relationship: I felt he wanted me to put pressure on my father on his behalf and I knew that wasn't right. He was constantly seeking reassurances from me and I didn't have the answers. After all, I was still trying to set up my side of the business.

But, Tony being Tony, he was determined to show me and my father that he could contribute something to Ann Summers, and when the parties kept running out of stock of one of our most successful lines, the penis mugs, he decided to step in and create a lucrative side-line for himself. The mugs were normal mugs, made in the Far East, but stuck right in the middle of them, inside, was a little china penis. They were enormously popular: people bought them as gifts or to serve tea to an unsuspecting guest – it was not until you had taken a few sips that you saw the top of this little white penis staring up at you. I should imagine there were a few scalded laps as Auntie Gladyses up and down the country dropped their mugs in horror and surprise!

Tony decided to try and find someone with a kiln to make the little china penises up for him to fit inside the mugs we had purchased. He started out by looking in the *Yellow Pages* and progressed from there. (He says that at one point he was so desperate he looked under W for Willy and P for Penis!) Eventually he found this young man with a kiln in Rotherhithe, south-east London, who was very amused and said he could take on the work. Well, as you can imagine, there were all sorts of disasters to start with. First the penises were too large and poked out over the mug tops, then they started to break away from the bottoms as soon as a hot drink was poured in. I don't think anyone ever swallowed one of them, but it certainly must come as a shock to find a penis floating in your cocoa.

We found the right formula in the end, but we had to order huge quantities of them to make it worth this chap's while. One night, after we had been to see him and were worried about the investment we had made, Tony and I were standing in the queue at a local McDonald's talking it over, when he suddenly turned and said to me in a loud voice: 'I don't know, Jack, here we are stuck with these ten thousand penises and we don't know what to do with them.' Well, the place went deadly quiet and we suddenly looked round and saw everyone staring at us in disbelief! Despite Tony's concerns, we did get rid of them all in the end and the chap we employed went on to design and make penis ashtrays which were also very popular.

At Ann Summers, meanwhile, things started to move really quickly. In 1982 I set up a telephone Orderline system, which can now take 100 orders every hour, but which had many teething problems to begin with. I desperately needed some help so I advertised for a junior and employed an eighteen-year-old girl called Caroline Johns (I was now twenty-one). She was great and had loads of enthusiasm, confidence and energy. She sat at the other end of my L-shaped desk.

I persuaded the board to give me more money because I realized that the product range and the catalogues were no longer suitable for our customers (although I was told that I would have to use as many of the old colour transparencies from the previous catalogue as possible to save money and time). In my opinion, they reflected the more seedy side of the business and there was too much emphasis on the marital aids and not enough on underwear. They were aimed at men more than women. When we asked the customers what they wanted, we found that there was a big discrepancy between what women wanted and what men wanted: for example, men liked women in black and women thought that men liked them in red and black; but, in reality, the women liked to wear white or pink.

I knew we had to concentrate on a range of pretty but sexy underwear that women would want to wear for themselves, as well as for their men. At this time we used two companies who acted as middlemen or suppliers. One was Romance Fashions, run by two little Jewish ladies who used to come to us with their garments, which were made using outworkers. The other company was Andre Paul, which was based in Essex. Ralph Gold was, and still is, a brilliant negotiator, so we went over to Andre Paul's together to buy some new items for the range. I remember that when we arrived a yellow Rolls-Royce was parked outside, which put Ralph off straight away because he said we must be paying him too much. The company had a showroom at the front of the building, and used outworkers like everyone else. I chose the items I wanted for the range and Ralph negotiated the price. I learned a great deal from him although several times I wanted to crawl under a desk because he was totally ruthless. I was inexperienced enough then to be embarrassed for the people we were trying to buy from!

Another project was to put the Ann Summers business on to computer, which required all new programming and stationery. I estimated that this would cost another £40,000. Also I wanted to run an advertising campaign in the South of England. Back I went to the board to explain all this. At this point we probably weren't making any money because I was cheating and using the Gold Star infrastructure to back up my side of the business. But there had been so much interest that it was obvious that the business was expanding rapidly and was worth investing in. By this time the board and I were holding regular monthly meetings for me to report on developments, but I didn't worry too much about persuading them: I knew it was in the bag.

After his success with the penis mugs Tony decided to get in on the act and help me to help myself. He came up with this idea of cutting out the lingerie middlemen and really making what Ann Summers wanted. He was never set up to replace the two other companies we were using, but to operate alongside them. As I saw it, this was an opportunity for him to be involved in the buzz and excitement of what I was achieving. He started off with the idea of producing crotchless knickers and G-strings and selling them to us. (Incidentally, I have often been described as the woman who put the G in G-string!) Everything was above board and I told him that if he could provide them at a cheaper rate than anywhere else, he would get the orders. Of course, there was a bit of insider dealing because he knew at that time how much the others were charging, but he still had to make them for less money and he was dealing directly with Ralph, which was no picnic.

After looking through the telephone directories for suppliers of materials, Tony and I found this sweet old lady called Jessie in the Commercial Road and we went up to her little shop and bought out all her trimmings. She became very fond of us and was always very warm and friendly when we went in there. Then we put an advert in the local paper in Biggin Hill for outworkers, and then I took over: I interviewed them all and made them do samples to show me that they could sew – we had about five. Tony would drive me round to pay them and pick up the garments. I also did all the stocktaking. D'Silva Designs was up and running. When it first started Tony was still working in the shops, which is why I had to do a lot of the work. But it soon got too much for me, so eventually he decided to leave the shops and run the business full-time on his own from home.

By this time I had brought into Ann Summers Kim Bond, who is still with me (as Sales Support Manager). She came in to handle the returns and do general admin work, but I also put her in charge of all the advertising. We were now using an agency and we asked them to monitor the adverts very carefully to see what conversion rate we were getting for our money – in other words which adverts were converting best into parties and new recruits.

Many of the local papers would not accept the adverts because of who we were. But, with those that did, we had phenomenal success. The *South London Press* was extremely successful, I remember, and we had a very good response from ads in the *Bristol Evening Post*. We were advertising simultaneously all around the country, but my big problem was that most of the organizers were in London and I was getting calls from people in Plymouth and Bristol but had no one to go and train them. So I decided to hire a training manager with a company car who could go down and set up all these women. I advertised locally and a very nice lady called Sandra Evans came to the interview. I explained the whole thing to her and, while we were talking, I noticed that she was looking at the nurse's uniform hanging up on the wall behind my desk. I didn't say anything, because I assumed she knew exactly what we were selling.

I was very impressed by her – she had worked for another Party Plan company called Oriflame – and I sent her away with a catalogue of our products. It was not until much later on that she told me she had assumed she was coming to work for a children's clothing company (hence the nurse's uniform), and it was only when she started to flick through the catalogue on the bus home that she realized what we sold and decided there and then that she definitely wanted to work for us! She eventually became Executive

Regional Manager, then left for a while to pursue her own business before coming back to work with us on a consultancy basis.

Sandra's job was to wait for a few women to respond to the advert in a particular area and make an appointment to go and see them all at the same time. She would train them up, issue them with kits and then manage them from London. We also recruited an in-house manager called Jayne Stevens, whose job was to look after the recruits in far-off places and go and see them once a month. At this time we would send the goods to them using the existing Gold Star distribution network, so we were delivering baby-doll nighties and vibrators to people's homes in great big HGV lorries! Later, we would just deliver from London to the depots and then a small delivery van would take the goods round to the organizers' homes.

We grew very rapidly during those first few months and had more than 1,000 organizers in the first year. Our first year's gross turnover was about £80,000. Around this time, with a team of about five staff helping me run it all, I moved departments again. I was delighted to see how it kept growing and growing. Even at that stage there were still cynics saying that it wouldn't last – it was just a fad – but I was getting good feedback and as my father's faith in me became more and more apparent, I had no reason to think it would fail. As I grew more knowledgeable and confident about the business the board's contribution diminished. This was particularly because the company was an all-women operation, with parties for women only, so the men on the board couldn't even have gone to a party if they wanted to and they just didn't really grasp the concept.

Right from the start it was my policy to recruit only women, and have the company run by women for women. Although initially we held some Ann Summers parties with men present (and one was even run by a man), these soon died out because the women felt uncomfortable buying such items from a man, and the husbands certainly didn't like the idea of men selling vibrators to their wives in their homes! As for male-only parties, which we also tried, they tended to be more like one-off stag nights and they didn't really take off.

With regard to our interviewing policy, I believe that with certain jobs you tend to attract a lot of women anyway, but in cases where a man did apply for a job with us, I would often prefer to employ a woman for a number of reasons. For example, when women customers ring in with their orders, they feel more comfortable ordering a stallion vibrator from another woman than from a man. I also desperately wanted to change the male-dominated image of the company, which caused me problems in the early stages because I was fire-fighting all the time. I knew that the company image was not attractive to women and I was trying to put that right, although I started out redressing the balance because there was really a need for all-women staff, as time went on and it became clear that men were not very keen on this all-women thing, I found it very satisfying. And I continually fight for that balance.

One incident which painfully brought male prejudice home to me was when one of the managers at work behaved in what I considered to be an offensive manner to a junior member of staff and to me, and was subsequently dismissed. He took his case to industrial tribunal and I regret to this day that I did not go and represent myself to the panel.

In my absence his dismissal was held to be unfair, and what really upset me was that the chairman of the panel commented that my 'delicate feelings should not have been hurt' and that I should have been used to being spoken to in that way, because some of the words that he used were printed in the books and magazines that Gold Star sold.

I was devastated. It was an insult to me, to my staff, to the 1,000 women in the field and their customers. What was the Chairman saying? That if you work in a pub you are an alcoholic? I was incensed by the whole affair – I felt patronized and insulted. It was only the first of many occasions when I have come up against male chauvinism and lost.

Chapter Four
SUMMER THE FIRST TIME

THE COMPANY I WAS now effectively running had already changed dramatically and was a million miles from the operation set up in 1970 by a rather eccentric character called Kim Caborn-Waterfield – known also during the Swinging Sixties as 'Dandy Kim'.

He was and still is a real character: he once dated Diana Dors and was rumoured to have gone out with Princess Margaret too. He was a man about town with a certain flair – he wrote an explicit sex manual under a pseudonym (published by his own Julian Press) and took bit-parts in films. It was he who came up with the idea of opening Britain's first sex supermarket 'for a laugh' and launched the first Ann Summers shop after seeing first-hand the success of the Beate Uhse chain of sex shops in Germany.

He decided on the name Ann Summers because of his affection for his secretary, Annice, who had adopted her stepfather's surname of Summers. The name conjured up an image of an English rose, which was just the thing for what he hoped would become the acceptable face of the British sex industry. The company logo of the heart-shaped apple with the bite out of it (to represent the forbidden fruit) was also Waterfield's idea. Annice was twenty-two – ten years younger than him – when they met in Chelsea; she was a very attractive blonde with 'great boobs and a warm personality' (his description) and later became his lover.

She moved into Waterfield's Jacobean house, Sedgehill Manor, and spoke afterwards of the enchanted life she led there with her flamboyant lover, who used to fly down to the Dorset estate in his helicopter 'signalling the start of a weekend of horses, good food and drink, pretty girls and amusing and attractive men'. The 'free love' ethos was very popular at Sedgehill. When he had money, Waterfield was undoubtedly a most generous host. But the creditors were constantly knocking on his door; apparently he once even hid his helicopter in a hay stack when the hire purchase company's officials came to repossess it.

Despite several previous business failures, Waterfield acquired the financial backing from friends like Robert Pilkington, of the Pilkington glass-manufacturing company, and set up the company Ann Summers Ltd, which he hoped would cash in on the increasingly liberal moral climate. His initial plan was to open a chain of 100 sex shops similar to the German chain, and set up an allied mail order operation for sex aids.

The first Ann Summers shop opened at 18 Edgware Road, next to the Odeon cinema at Marble Arch, in September 1970. It featured an airy, open-plan design, wall-to-wall carpet and piped music. There was so much publicity and public interest on the opening day that commissionaires had to be employed outside to manage the queues. The press were there in force: newspaper reporters, television camera crews, and photographers; Annice opened the champagne and toasted 'love, sex and happiness, in and out of marriage'. Her high-cheekboned features appeared in every tabloid newspaper and on television newsreels throughout the country and around the world.

She became a sort of agony aunt to dozens of customers who came into her shop seeking advice on how to spice up their sex lives. She recommended particular products to the sexually impotent or dormant and gently led them through the maze of marital aids. In one classic example of the naivety of some of our earlier customers, a woman being shown the 'D' Spray ('D' for 'Delay'), which was supposed to hold a man's erection for longer and delay ejaculation, was advised that it might make her lips numb. In complete innocence she asked the member of staff: 'Why on earth would I want to spray it on my lips?'

Another customer, an American woman who was desperate for a vibrator, rang up Ann Summers headquarters and asked where she could buy one. She was told about the new store in Marble Arch and expressed her relief. 'Thank God for Ann Summers!' she said. 'I have recently had a hormone implant and the damn thing is working already, just as my husband has gone abroad on business for a month!'

Despite the favourable reception by the national media and the shop's earliest customers, public outrage at the nation's first sex supermarket soon reached epic proportions. The Midlands, in particular, rallied its mothers and clergy against the threat of a sex shop there. In Bristol there was an evangelical protest march against the chain, and the moral matrons of the Home Counties recruited their forces through the Women's Institute. Annice spear-headed the damage limitation exercise herself and toured the country, calming nerves and reassuring the Mary Whitehouse brigade. As part of the PR exercise, she travelled with a troupe of attractive young women who handed out red apples to bemused passers-by.

With her soft voice and clipped upper-class accent, Annice seemed to allay the fears of the moral majority and belied people's image of the company; soon she became a popular national figure. A former secretary, she was very inexperienced and was delighted with all the attention she received. Because of her high profile, Waterfield encouraged her to take a more active role in the company, and the shop in particular. What neither of them realized was that although the shop was designed to cash in on the sexual revolution, few women were actually ready to walk into a sex shop and buy marital aids.

However, initially, it was very successful, reaping Waterfield something like £5,000 a week in the first few weeks. Afraid that if it were known Dandy Kim was involved the company would lose a lot of its support, he kept a deliberately low profile and let Annice run the show. Through her, he announced his ambitious expansion plans, but he opened only one more shop in Bristol before things started to go badly wrong. Annice was really quite ahead of her time in many ways, and she saw this as a great personal opportunity. She had big plans for the future that weren't always commercial. The initial surge of interest died down and fell away, but the crunch came when the company branched out into mail order shortly before a postal strike, which brought it to its knees. Money and goods were locked in post boxes and Waterfield was unable to retrieve them. Annice resigned in 1971 after acrimonious discussions with Waterfield over money and promptly sold her story to the *News of the World*, exposing him for the first time as the man behind the entire venture.

Shortly afterwards Ann Summers went into voluntary liquidation with nearly £90,000 worth of debts (equivalent to more than £1,800,000 today). Without the intervention of my father and Ralph, the company might well have sunk without a trace.

Gold Star had been one of the suppliers to the Ann Summers shops from the beginning, providing books, novelties and magazines. It was a relatively small but promising outlet for the company, so when Ann Summers went into receivership, David and Ralph found themselves with an unpaid bill of about £1,500 (about £30,000 in today's money). By this time they had moved to their new headquarters in Whyteleafe (Gadoline House was named after a tiny company they bought years before which proved to have a very useful tax loss they discovered they could carry forward!). Reluctant as ever to miss an opportunity, David and Ralph decided to buy Waterfield out.

It was 1971 and they bought Ann Summers (the shops and the name) for £10,000 (now approximately £200,000), along with the debts. They were happy; Waterfield was certainly happy when he walked away from the deal; Annice was asked to come back and manage the shops. She was, after all, the face of Ann Summers.

I was only eleven years old and knew nothing of the purchase, but my father now tells me that they were quite excited by it because it was an entirely new move for them. Since the split from Goddy they had largely abandoned High Street retailing and had concentrated on the publishing side of the business. Now, they thought, it made sense to keep this controversial and widely publicized shop open, buy the name of Ann Summers Ltd and have it trading under a company they owned called Lydcare, and diversify a little. Their company was doing well (it must have been to fork out nearly £1 million), and they felt that the time was right. Ralph negotiated the deal and it seemed a fair price.

Keen to keep the momentum of the Ann Summers name going, they quickly bought a third shop in Queensway, West London, and put Annice in charge of that. The launch, on 11 May 1972, once again attracted widespread media interest and Annice was photographed smiling at the cash register in front of a poster of a topless model and next to a rack of love potion called Action Cream. My father recalls: 'Annice was good for PR, or was certainly perceived to be. She had basic merchandising skills and all the attributes required. We were pleased to have her on board because selling sex aids was still a very delicate business in those days. We were just emerging from the Dark Ages to a barefoot and pregnant type of image, and she was helping bring it out of that era.'

The Gold brothers left Annice alone for the first few months, expecting her to put her experience from the early days of Marble Arch to good use. But when the first month's figures started coming in and were largely disappointing, they travelled to London to see how she was getting along. They discovered, to their horror, that the new shop was very different from the previous two, rather softer and more feminine. The friction increased when Annice insisted that she knew what was right. My father and Ralph recall that everything she proposed to them was 'non-negotiable' and they found her increasingly difficult to work with.

My father accused Annice of trying to go up-market, moving

away from the sex supermarket idea to Janet Reger-style lingerie, and abandoning the basic principle of the shop's success. She failed to understand that the market was still entirely male-dominated at this time and that the Gold brothers, of all people, knew the sex business. They were not happy to be forking out money for that sort of operation, especially when the sales figures showed that their almost exclusively male customers were only interested in buying the baby-doll and black-lace numbers for their wives or girlfriends.

Because Annice had been placed on something of a pedestal by the press and by Waterfield, I think she must have started to believe that she was in a position to influence Ralph and David. She had appeared on television chat shows and in 1972 she was even voted 'Woman of the Year' by the London *Evening Standard*, but she had no real business background. She suddenly started to demand things the company could not afford and had no intention of funding. I think she may have felt frustrated and angry with the Gold brothers because they were not giving her the respect and attention she was accustomed to. And from my own experience with them, I knew how cautious they were about investing new money.

After several clashes with Annice over a period of six months, Dad and Ralph sold the Queensway shop (making a substantial profit at the peak of a property boom) and closed it down. She resigned and went to France. Despite all Waterfield's early promises of a stake in the business, she had no shareholdings; she was merely a figurehead. Although ahead of her time, I think she was just too young and idealistic to make any business or commercial sense out of the operation. It was a shame for both her and Waterfield because they had, for a short while, tasted fame and fortune and neither of them wanted to relinquish it.

Soon after she left, my father and uncle heard that she was involved in a terrible car accident in France and was quite severely injured. Fortunately, she recovered and after that she met an American millionaire and was last heard of happily married with homes in Italy, America and London. She is one of the people I would really like to meet. I don't know how she would feel towards me after her dealings with my father and uncle, but I am fascinated by her involvement in Ann Summers at its inception, and one day I would love to sit down over tea and talk to her about it all. She must be well into her forties by now.

After he was bought out Kim Caborn-Waterfield pursued a number of other business ventures – some of them indirectly involving the Gold brothers – but he then disappeared from the scene for quite some while. He was never employed by the Golds, and had nothing further to do with the shops or Party Plan; he set up different projects with people and sought financial backing. Later on he also had shares in one of the Gold Group's telephone chat-line companies.

We heard nothing from him for several years, by which time I had gained a higher profile with Ann Summers. Then *Cosmopolitan* magazine ran an article about me; Kim Caborn-Waterfield saw it and took offence. It must have been because I said something about there never being a real Ann Summers, it had just been a name Waterfield had chosen – which, strictly speaking is true. Annice existed, of course, but she was someone for Waterfield to hide behind. Having read this and seen my rise to fame and fortune, Waterfield must have felt a bit like the fifth Beatle; he felt left out and wanted more credit for the success of the company.

No one can ever take away from Waterfield the fact that he started the whole thing going, thought of the name and opened the first shop. It was he who set Ann Summers on its way to becoming a household name. But the Party Plan idea was not his – nor was the concept mine originally – and I very much doubt if he had even heard of it; it was something that housewives took part in. Ten years after he had been in financial difficulty and the Gold brothers had bailed him out, I came up with the idea of introducing Party Plan to Ann Summers; I persuaded the board to let me set it

Aged six I accompany my parents on a business trip to New York in 1966. Mum disliked flying, so we went aboard the *Queen Elizabeth*, and the trip took four days each way.

Above: My marriage to Tony D' Silva on 2 August 1980.

Left: Rosie Gold, my grandmother, pictured after her eighty-first birthday. Rosie still works every day in her shop opposite West Ham football ground.

Above: Blonde Annice Summers provided the company name in 1970.

Left: The Ann Summers store at Marble Arch, London in the early '80s. The windows were blacked out at the request of the local council.

Opposite: Ann Summers catalogue 14 depicts my sister Vanessa (far right) in her early modelling days.

Ann Summers

Summer Catalogue No. 14

Emanuelle

Rochelle

Nicole

Above: Opening a store in Croydon in April 1995. The store design had just been radically updated to reflect our new retailing concept.

Left: One of my favourite photos: me (right) and Vanessa in 1994.

Above: Denise Bonner, National Sales Executive, Julie Harris, Sales Director, Jacqueline Gold and Sandra Evans, Area Manager (pictured left to right).

Above: Xcalibur, one of the two raunchy Ann Summers dance troupes. Performing regularly in the UK and overseas, their show lasts around 40 minutes.

Left: I open the 1994 Annual General Conference with the firm support of dance troupe Xcalibur.

Me and Matthew Kelly at the Hotel de France, Jersey, celebrating Ann Summers' tenth anniversary.

Me and Stuart.
(© Brian Aris)

The changing style of Ann Summers 1983 and 1995.

up and follow it through and there is no way that he can claim any of the credit for that.

At about the same time as the *Cosmo* article appeared, I was preparing for our Ten-Year Conference and I decided to do a 'This is Your Life' type of presentation about the company. Mandy Boosey, our Design Studio Manager, who was researching and organizing this, innocently and without my knowledge wrote to Kim Caborn-Waterfield in September 1991 asking him for information. This is what really started him off. Shortly afterwards he wrote back, saying that he was unable to help and informing us that he was planning to write a book about the first twenty-one years of the company and wanted access to personnel, photographs and files. I was horrified at the thought. How could he write a book about Ann Summers when he didn't know Ann Summers any more? I didn't know this man but my back was up already. My father and I sat down and discussed how we were going to play it.

Ralph met Waterfield first and suggested that he might like to consider a deal whereby the book became a joint venture. The meeting did not go well and thereafter my father and I dealt directly with him. Waterfield said he was determined to go ahead with the book and was keen not to have any inaccuracies in it, although he admitted that it would be very critical. I knew that any information he had about the company must be coming from someone inside, and I had my suspicions.

My father and I took him to lunch at a restaurant near his home in Battersea, and it seemed to take all day. He sat there in his denim shirt and jeans telling us all about the books he had written and the films he had produced and the people he knew. He finally came to the point: his wonderful book, which would be about my life and his life. His intention seemed to be to get our co-operation, but he was so carried away with himself that we never moved beyond the general points.

I knew we had to have another meeting with Waterfield, which I was not looking forward to. I arranged for a car to bring him to a local restaurant. Once again I sat gritting my teeth through two hours of waffle. Finally he came back to the subject of the book. He said it would be about me, and that I would have a clothes budget and be glamorized and promoted like Annice had been. I told him that we did not want a book about Ann Summers. He said he was going to write the book anyway, his way, and he estimated that he would make about £180,000 from it. I considered offering him money for the rights to the book to ensure it wasn't published, but the price was too high. He added, for good measure, that he wanted me to employ his daughter, who was out of work.

Waterfield had come to this meeting with the manuscript he had been working on for eight months — it was a very thin file of scrappy bits of paper. Now that I knew how little he had, I was very relieved. But I didn't give anything away; I sat and listened and paid the bill and agreed to stay in touch and then we left.

I had been very concerned by the first meeting because I was understandably protective of Ann Summers and Party Plan: it was at its peak and doing brilliantly and I didn't want anything to spoil it. I learned a lot from my father during that meeting. One of his sayings is that you have nothing to fear but fear itself, and he was so calm and collected. I had waited patiently to see what it was that Waterfield had to say, but by the end of the second meeting it was very clear to me what I had to do. Back at the office I asked myself if there really would be a book. Having seen his little file, I decided to call his bluff. Waterfield had given us a detailed synopsis of the book and I asked a solicitor to look at it. I was told that the synopsis was already defamatory. He claimed that I told Chris and Ann — the two women who bought the Ann Summers underwear to sell at the original parties — that I wanted to get rid of them because they were Cockneys and too common to fit in with the new company image. This was absolute rubbish: they may have (wrongly) assumed that, but they eventually left the company of their own accord and not because I tried to get rid of them.

My own father is a Cockney, my grandparents are genuine East

Enders; I am not a snob and never have been. If I were a snob I would have given up the sex aids side of the business and concentrated on the lingerie for the more up-market type of customer, but housewives are our bread and butter, and I am proud of that. Another part of the synopsis referred to the parties and was headlined 'Fu—erware' – a play, presumably, on the word 'Tupperware', which I thought was insulting.

After the second meeting I decided that we would not have anything more to do with Waterfield. Since then, the affair has been dealt with through solicitors' letters, including one in 1992 which told Waterfield:

> Our clients can only conclude from your conduct so far that you are motivated by the basest of commercial considerations and that you are preparing to publish this attack on our clients in order to make profits at our clients' expense. In view of this, we must put you on notice that our clients reserve the right to claim exemplary damages in the proceedings which we are instructed to commence in the event that you continue with the decision to publish a libel of them.

Another letter warned Waterfield that one proposed chapter he had sent us contained 'inaccuracies, half-truths, distortions and innuendoes' and was defamatory. After an initial flurry of letters, we didn't hear from him again for a while, but a couple of articles appeared – one in *Private Eye*, in which he claimed that he had been beaten up in the street and implied that the Gold brothers had arranged it because he had written this book and they didn't like it.

In October 1993 a big article on Waterfield (entitled DANDY KIM AND THE GIRLIE MAG MILLIONAIRES) appeared in the *Mail on Sunday*. He had apparently demanded a modelling fee for the photograph and the article described him as 'vaguely comical at sixty-three in tight jeans and cowboy boots'. It referred to his own conviction in France for the theft of $25,000 from American film producer Jack Warner, an allegation which has always been vehemently denied by Kim Waterfield, and alluded to the property companies, beach bar and water-skiing school that had all gone bust under his ownership and the helicopter that had been repossessed.

The worst that Waterfield could come up with was that I was the 'photogenic front-girl for an operation based on sleazy international trade in pornography', and that David and Ralph were 'porn barons' – which seems to be the press's favourite cliché for them. They sold girlie magazines, he said. This had, of course, been common knowledge for years. We have never been ashamed of that or tried to hide it. And after all, Waterfield had himself been in the sex industry.

He also repeated the suggestions he had made in *Private Eye* about being beaten up, on which the *Mail on Sunday* commented: 'Although there is no evidence whatsoever that these events are in any way linked with either the Golds or his book, he waves about police reports on the incidents and shows photographs of his badly bruised eye.' The article also, thankfully, suggested that the whole story might be a bluff to frighten 'lascivious housewives' into dropping out of Ann Summers, and said that Waterfield would 'like nothing better' than to have an injunction slapped on his book to increase publicity and press interest.

After that it all seemed to fizzle out and the expected book didn't materialize. My father, once again, was right: we did have nothing to fear.

Incidentally, on the 'porn baron' question, I should like to clear up a few points. Of course there have been times when it has crossed my mind to divorce myself totally from the Gold Group because of the constant media focus on the Gold Star side – the part which publishes, distributes and sells soft-porn magazines. But generally speaking I have always felt that it was better to be upfront about it and tell people exactly what the Gold Group does, from printing T-shirts to selling puzzle magazines. Gold Star is one of twenty companies within the group, and the girlie mags are a very small part of it.

I think people have lurid visions of what we sell. Gold Star produces eight separate puzzle magazines, including *Word Finder*, *Letter Fit* and *Puzzle Library*, and about forty soft-porn magazines, whose titles range from *New Direction* and *Continental* to *Torrid* and *Lesbian Lust*. We also have titles such as *Milkmaids*, *Rustler Fantasy*, *Swish*, *Journal of Love*, *Derriere*, *Dick Rambone* and *Cheeky*. They are nothing more than soft porn; they are not illicit publications which feature people having sex with animals or children. No one openly or legitimately sells that type of hard-core pornography, and my family would never want to be involved with it. People are often quite surprised to find that, as a family, the Golds actually have a strict moral code and are quite prim and proper. The very 'worst' of the magazines we sell are for top shelves of newsagents shops; they are all strictly within the law as ruled by the Obscene Publications Act and they cater to a huge market that would exist with or without our input. It is many years since the Obscene Publications Squad has felt the need to raid our premises or investigate our products.

The magazines are often accused of exploiting women, but my view is that the male and female models have voluntarily gone into this kind of work and often make a great deal of money from it. Many of them go on to become household names by appearing on page three of the *Sun* or in the *Daily Sport*. Pornographic magazines are bought by people from all backgrounds and classes, with diverse views on women and sexuality. Those who regard women as nothing more than sex objects generally feel that way because of circumstances in their lives and not because they read soft-porn magazines.

As for the titles for people who enjoy sado-masochistic activities like bondage, fetishism, spanking and domination, there is a market out there and we cater for it. It doesn't turn me on – or my father, as far as I know – but if that is what some people want then that is entirely up to them. We also openly sell the goods they require to satisfy their tastes – blow-up dolls (male and female), whips, rubber- and leather-wear, handcuffs, masks, underwear with various attachments and latex wear.

My attitude to the magazines is surely much like any other woman's: I find them rather seedy and full of unattractive people. Often the men who read them don't seem to be worried about the quality of the people they are looking at. I think women are far more critical. What offends me about them more than anything – more than the stories or the spreads of the girls – is the lack of balance: the men are not allowed to have an erection, while the women reveal all. These magazines are for men, who can already go into a strip show or a sex shop or visit a prostitute to satisfy all their sexual needs; not only is there hardly an equivalent magazine for women, but – worst of all – some of the men who read these magazines and have all these fantasies claim that women wouldn't even want one. I felt I wanted to redress the balance.

When I started Party Plan my initiative was financed by the group, and some of that money came from girlie magazines, among many other entirely respectable things. What I have been able to do with that money is to get the balance right: to create something for women, run by women and with women's needs and desires in mind. I have actually created a reverse situation – a company and a product range with which men often feel as uncomfortable as women do with the girlie magazines.

Of course I would like to see the Gold Star magazines go more up-market because that is what I personally find more appealing. And there are many other changes I would like to make in the way the company markets some of its other products. But even when I am Chairperson of the Gold Group, if the magazines are still making money then they stay. There is nothing in the range that I would consider deeply offensive and I am generally entirely comfortable with the product. I am a businesswoman, and I make commercial decisions for the good of my company and my staff and not just because some people might find me morally more palatable if I did something else. What I would like and what would be viable are sometimes two different things. I have responsibilities and duties to a great many people and if that one small part of the group, which makes a respectable amount of money, means that the rest of the group stays healthy then I am not going to start getting prudish.

As for Kim Caborn-Waterfield, the *Mail on Sunday* article was not, unfortunately, the last I heard of him. In May 1995 a copy of his final manuscript was dropped on to my desk – a 135-page diatribe against the Golds and how they had made their money. He planned to publish a paperback himself for £4.99, using the Julian Press again. This was to be the first of a 'series' of books and his story would bring in money from newspapers and television documentary companies – he claimed he already had a serialization with a Sunday tabloid newspaper. The manuscript rambled dreadfully – it was like sitting at the dinner table with him again – and he detailed his preparations for the legal action he expected us to take.

I read it right through and thought how sad it was that this man in his sixties should still be harping on about how he had somehow missed out on my success. He gave me no credit at all for setting up Party Plan and suggested that if my father and Ralph hadn't decided to turn me into the new Annice, I would have had a career as a model in one of their magazines. I honestly didn't know whether to laugh or cry!

After giving the matter serious consideration and getting advice from our lawyers, I decided not to take any direct action and to wait and see whether he managed to sell any copies of what we considered to be an obsessive account of events based on testimony from disillusioned former staff. I suspect not and we watch with interest to see whether any newspaper would be foolish enough to serialize it. Even though we know exactly what happened and why, and all those who really know us believe in us whole-heartedly, I can only hope that the people who matter – the party organizers, customers and general public who might go into one of our shops – will see this man for what he is.

Chapter Five
GROWING PAINS

I N 1982, WHEN THE Party Plan concept had really
started to take off, Chris Rogers and Ann Galea – who were
by this time managers in their areas with massive units of
more than sixty women each – came to me and told me they
wanted a piece of the action. At this stage they were earning
more than I was because of all the recruits they had (we have since
decided that the ideal unit size is twelve, with twenty as a
maximum, otherwise the unit cannot be properly managed, but I
didn't have enough managers then and was still going through a
learning curve).

So here they were – two women who were earning all this money
on a percentage of their organizers' sales: they no longer had to
hold many parties themselves – claiming they deserved a percentage of the whole business. They suggested that it was something
they had been promised, by way of a verbal agreement, but I had
certainly never said anything of the kind.

Party Plan, they said, was all their idea. My attitude was then –
and is now – that while I have always given them full credit for the
scheme to sell Ann Summers goods at Pippa Dee parties, no idea is
original. We all seek opportunities and gain inspiration from
others, and what they did was to utilize Pippa Dee's concept to their
own advantage. Pippa Dee had, in turn, taken the Party Plan idea
from Tupperware. I had taken all those ideas one stage further and
turned them into a success.

The percentage Chris and Ann were asking for meant that they
would effectively be owning shares in the company, yet there had

been no financial burden on their part and their earning potential was already limitless. They had not had to sit in front of the board and make a presentation; they had not paced the bedroom floor at night trying to work out in which direction the company should move next and how the board was to be persuaded it would work. They had just taken on more and more recruits until they were unable to run them properly, but they were too inexperienced to be area managers. I said no to them, because as far as I was concerned they were already on to a very good earning opportunity.

I didn't have full financial control of the company until early 1983, but by now this decision was mine alone. The board involvement had largely dropped away – some of them didn't honestly know the difference between a pair of French knickers and a body. I would hear them in innocent conversation about something to do with Ann Summers and I knew they had it all wrong. They thought they knew what we were selling and why women went to these parties, but despite their business acumen, they didn't, because it was a very female thing.

Shortly after Chris and Ann had approached me, a company in North London called Silver Rose, run by a man called Geoff Silver, came on to the scene. He had one shop selling erotic underwear and a mail order catalogue but no Party Plan scheme; he just advertised in *Exchange & Mart* and other magazines. Silver Rose made the two ladies an offer to set up their own Party Plan shortly after our meeting and they resigned and left. They told me they had been given a better offer elsewhere. They didn't take very many ladies with them – about thirty – but it was quite a shock coming at such a crucial time in our development. It was still very early days for us – we were still growing and I hadn't really foreseen this problem. However, I realized that I had to give my staff the confidence to get over the setback and move forward. There wasn't much we could do about it, but I tried to build up morale, saying that we had to fight it, and pointing out that the grass was not always greener.

The senior organizers, particularly, took the desertion very personally. They felt utterly let down by the women who had defected or were thinking about it, and were very upset. I drove down to visit as many as I could – I didn't have the time to see them all – in an effort to persuade them to remain with us. It was hard to sit in their homes trying to talk them into staying, knowing that they had probably already made up their minds. I won some and I lost some.

Still, losing organizers then was not a disaster because it was in the days when we were still picking up around thirty new recruits a day. It was later on, after other poaching attempts, that it mattered more. What happened later, in 1989, with a company called Lovelace really demotivated me. I felt as if I were seeing everything disintegrate before my eyes. We had really never experienced such heavy and direct poaching before, and although I tried to find comfort in boosting company morale and trying to bolster my own, it was very difficult. I just kept telling my team that at the end of the day we were the best and would continue to be the best.

It all started after I employed someone to take over control of the organizers in the North of England. We were doing so well in the South, I knew we had to start advertising in the North too, which was really Party Plan country. But it would have been foolish to start advertising up there – it was a long way away and I didn't have anyone to deal with the responses. John Gibbins knew of someone called Joyce Greenhill who was in the Tupperware Party Plan business; he thought it would be a good idea to set her up in the North, so she came to work for us in May 1983. She dressed smartly and spoke intelligently but she was very overbearing but in its own way that achieved results. She was also very knowledgeable and I needed that, so I took her on and she made a valuable contribution to our plans for the North. All she had to do was train a few people up and show them how to recruit and it all expanded very quickly.

But as I strove to improve the image of the company and Joyce achieved executive status – which she had admittedly earned – the company outgrew her. We were moving into a more sophisticated, professional arena and I was looking to groom senior people for top jobs. She didn't seem to fit in with that image. I remember shortly after we had been invited to join the Direct Selling Association, we were invited to our first proper conference at which Michael Heseltine was present. Joyce was very keen to stand up and say something and I kept telling her to sit down and be quiet. I was really worried about what she might do because the conference was being held in front of the Minister for Trade & Industry and finally, during a workshop discussion, she could hold back no longer. She stood up and in a loud voice suggested that the other members there should follow our lead in encouraging our ladies by giving them each a penis pencil as a gift with their raffle tickets. This was ten years ago and the DSA were not ready for talk about penis pencils. I prayed for the ground to swallow me up – I actually felt myself slide down in my chair. There was a long silence and then the meeting swiftly moved on. Afterwards some of the members came over and commiserated with me; apparently I had looked deeply uncomfortable.

It became more and more apparent to me that Joyce was not adapting to the new company approach. We were becoming a lot more structured but Joyce didn't seem to like all the new formalities. I think she also felt threatened by other women, like Sandra Evans, who were coming up through the ranks. I was actively promoting such people for their sophistication and professionalism, as I became more sophisticated and professional myself.

At this time Lovelace were operating by mail order from Addington with a shop in George Street, Croydon. It was run by a man called Carl Slack. Lovelace had been minor rivals but they suddenly became a major threat. Joyce came to me one day and told me she had been approached by Carl Slack and had been wined and dined and flattered; apparently he wanted to poach her from us. She was obviously feeling insecure: she asked me to match what Lovelace were offering her, and she wanted a flash car and a directorship of the company. I realised at this point that our objectives differed.

I believe very strongly that people have to earn their colours. I had had to earn mine and, without underestimating what she had achieved in the North, I knew Joyce was not ready for a directorship. It was a very difficult decision for me to make. I risked letting her go knowing that she would take the ladies who were loyal to her in the North. Lovelace were trying to do the same thing up there and I realized it would cause us problems, but in the end I decided it was the lesser of two evils. I also resented being blackmailed.

I turned her down and she went to work for Lovelace in September 1988. Needless to say, the poaching campaign began: it started in Area 6 – Newcastle – in about March 1989. At that time we had no confidentiality clauses saying that the organizers couldn't work for rival companies, which is usual now within Party Plan.

Joyce went mad poaching our organizers. I had lots of crisis meetings with the area managers – I don't recall losing any women at that level, but we did lose a lot of those who were working under them. I set up a campaign of damage limitation with the area managers, trying to win the organizers round. I warned them that Lovelace would make them false promises, all on condition that they brought their unit with them. Once Lovelace had the units, then it would be goodbye, because they would not be needed any more. Most important, I told the senior organizers that, no matter how bitter or let down they felt, they had to make sure that the ladies who went left on good terms – that they felt they could come back. I told the team that our organizers were, in effect, customers, not employees, and should have a right to go elsewhere if they wanted to. I sent a letter to all the defectors saying that although we were obviously disappointed, the door was always open at Ann Summers and they were welcome to return. None the less, Lovelace did a lot of damage, not just to Ann Summers but also to the industry as a whole. I think we lost about 500 organizers to them, which was a huge number.

Party Plan is not the easy make it appears to be — you can't just jump on the bandwagon: I had learned that the hard way. I knew that it would not be long before Carl Slack realized he had made a huge mistake taking Joyce Greenhill on. Less than a year later I approached Lovelace because I had heard things were not going well. I invited Carl Slack down and offered to buy his business. Papers were drawn up and I arranged a meeting at Lovelace's premises to finalize the deal and take the ladies over. In May 1990 the meeting was held over lunch with Carl Slack and his executives, including Joyce Greenhill. It was a polite but tense encounter. Joyce was looking to get her job back but under no circumstances would I even contemplate reinstating her.

We negotiated a good deal based on a percentage of the ladies, but in actual fact they never came back in droves as we had hoped because after the Lovelace experience they were fed up with Party Plan. Only a handful of the organizers came back, but some were first-class operators and are still with us today. So in the end we didn't get very much out of the deal, although we did stop the poaching. That experience taught me that you have to act quickly in fighting off rivals who try to take over your business.

Funnily enough, after the deal was all sorted out Carl became a very good friend of Ralph's, despite all that had happened. He still runs a mail order business, and as part of the deal we agreed to purchase from his lingerie-manufacturing business.

At the age of twenty-six, I was quickly acquiring the management skills I needed — I don't know whether some of them were inherited from my father. I have always read a great many self-improvement books and articles about successful people. I like to think up different ideas and put them into effect and this was a very productive and creative period of my life.

I was also constantly inspired by my father, and our relationship was improving all the time. I think he was enjoying my success, and thinking that this mousy young girl of his had grown into a promising businesswoman. He was much more approachable and easy to talk to and he had a very calming influence on me. I tended to overreact and panic at this stage, but Dad's saying about nothing to fear but fear itself held me steady on many occasions. At moments of crisis or decision, I would simply remember those words and say to myself: 'He is right, you have to come to terms with this and be positive,' and I think my own business philosophy has evolved from that.

Even now I find that problems motivate me as well as successes. They all lead to further opportunities. I find the conferences of the Direct Selling Association very inspiring. I looked up to people there and held them in very high regard, although I felt that we were rather cold-shouldered to start with because of who we were. People seemed very apprehensive about welcoming us. I had very little support and encouragement from other members in those early days, but in some ways that was good for me because, having accepted that I lacked experience and needed help, the only thing I could do was to listen to the customers to see what they wanted.

Armed with this pioneering market research, I implemented systems to deal with the problems – systems that were new and unique. I had no choice but to work it all out for myself. At one time I had considered my inexperience a weakness, but it turned out to be our greatest advantage.

When we were first invited to join the DSA, which was quite an honour, Paul Southworth, the President of Avon and someone I admired very much, asked me to speak at the next conference. At first I wasn't sure if I wanted to do it, but I knew that if I didn't I was going to stand still. This was important for my own self-development. I had overcome most of my nerves by this time, but I was understandably keen to create the right impression in front of 150 people – mainly men – with all their preconceived ideas about

Ann Summers. They knew we were fairly successful but I had attended other conferences and seen the heckling that sometimes went on.

I spent ages preparing a twenty-five-minute speech. The DSA wanted to know about our success because we were a bit of a mystery; at that time we hadn't had much press coverage. I really wanted the speech to be good — I have always been a perfectionist. As I was called up to the podium the room went deathly silent: everyone was very curious. I had to be careful in choosing my slides — sometimes one becomes immune to one's own products and I didn't want to offend anyone. I think I concentrated on the lingerie range — I certainly avoided showing them photographs of vibrators or anything like that. The only time I had a reaction was when I told them how men all say they once 'bought something for a friend', and they all nodded and laughed as if I had struck a nerve. When I announced our turnover figures you could hear the shocked response. People had completely underestimated our professionalism and size, so they were astounded when I mentioned a figure with a 'million' after it.

Afterwards people made a point of seeking me out: I was asked if we really relied on feedback from our customers and if we really had an all-woman team? I remember someone asking me if that helped the business — he was in cosmetics and had not one woman on his executive team.

I use the DSA to dispel some of the myths about Ann Summers and the company's background. I have come up against so much prejudice in my career that it is now a big issue for me — not that my experiences are anything compared to those of my father and uncle: they had to struggle through the moral high ground of the sixties and seventies. I have never been taken to court, like my father and Ralph, although once I was almost arrested.

It was in August 1985, when we were exhibiting at the Woman's World Exhibition in Bristol. There were stands with everything from cosmetics and bridal wear to household goods. We thought it would be a perfect opportunity for us to promote ourselves in the West Country. We booked a stand – very much on a shoe-string budget – and went down to set it up ourselves: me, Tony and a designer called Angela Bailey and some of the other staff who were to man the stand during the week.

The stand was like a room that you could walk into and was decked out in pink. We pinned lingerie to the outer part – this was my chance at last to fulfil my childhood ambition to be a window dresser – and we made a little private cubicle within the stand with a shelf on it to display the sex aids, which were all pretty harmless actually – just a range of our best-selling vibrators. It was almost like a changing room and no one could go in there unless they were over eighteen; they could see and hold the items, but were not allowed to try them out!

The idea was to promote the parties, not to sell anything. BBC Radio West asked if they could interview me at the stand and although I had never really dealt with the media before, I agreed because I thought it would be good publicity. They came and recorded the interview and played it later in the day on prime time radio; I thought it went very well. That first day was amazing: Lewis Collins of the TV programme *"The Professionals"* opened the event and actually came on to our stand to have a look around. I gave him a willy warmer to take home. Tony handed out catalogues to people walking past and the stand was very popular. A lot of people, it seemed, had heard the radio programme, including the local police.

The next thing I knew was these two plainclothes officers had appeared; one of them asked me who was running the stand. I told him I was and he said he was going to have to arrest me for running a sex shop without a licence. I still didn't have very much confidence then and this was the first time I had ever been confronted with the police: I was absolutely terrified, but I was also furious. I stood my ground, and I told the senior officer that I wasn't running a sex shop because I wasn't selling anything and didn't need a licence. I didn't actually know if that was true or not (it was, in fact) but I thought I would try it on. He did seem a little thrown by that – I could see him hesitate. But then he decided to call my bluff and said that he would be back the following day, and if I hadn't removed my stand he would arrest me, and off he went. The younger officer could see that I was shaken by that because before he left he said he was sure it would be O.K.

Tony and Angela stood there in disbelief and we all watched them go. I nearly sank to my knees at that point; I had been convinced that I was going to be marched off to the cells there and then. Sick with worry over what might happen, I called my father for moral support. He was great and gave me the benefit of his advice and reassurance, although he did say he thought what happened next was very much down to the individual officer. I told him that I wasn't going to give in, that I was prepared to go to prison if I had to because I was sure that I was right.

The next morning I was at the stand early and was pacing up and down all day. I can't remember if I packed my toothbrush or not, but I was all prepared to be locked up. Well, of course the policemen never came back and the stand stayed up all week and was a great success. But I don't think I fully relaxed until we had packed it all away and were heading home up the motorway.

It was in 1984 that I was contacted by an organizer called Lynda Schofield who was being transferred with her soldier husband to a British army base in Düsseldorf, Germany. She asked if she could take her kit out there and start selling Ann Summers goods to the women in the camps. I said yes, and once she started to get orders we posted the goods out to her. At first she held parties for British women, but then news of them started filtering through to the German nationals and we quickly realized that there was so much interest we would have to produce some catalogues in German. Lynda was out there for a couple of years and helped us to set it all up. When she came back here we promoted an area manager – an English woman who spoke fluent German.

We then started to recruit German women and they were very successful with the parties. We now have a German Area Manager, Marion Foster, who has a team of German nationals under her. The British Forces business diminished as the camps disappeared, but the German business has flourished. It also became our introduction to Holland because the Germans were only a few hours from the Dutch border; before long the women were holding parties in Holland too. Realizing that the German organizers were having to return to Germany to bank their money, we set up properly in Holland. We now have an office in Germany, in München-Gladbach, one in Holland and one in Denmark. There are about 300 organizers in each country.

We have discovered that European women have different requirements to British women. They have no particular interest in the sex aids because they have sex shops coming out of their ears, and we obviously don't sell them any of the English books. They are more interested in the garments and prefer more covered lingerie with frilly lace and bows. The Germans are very business-like and look upon a party as a shopping opportunity rather than a fun night out. Perhaps it is the slightly giggly, rather ribald attitude to sex in Britain that makes Ann Summers so successful here.

It is surprisingly hard breaking into a foreign market and we have never had the success we would have liked. Problems were not exclusively Continental, either. I remember the difficulties we had, first with Eire and then with Guernsey and the customs officers there. They have quite strict moral laws in the Channel Islands; they even banned the Chippendales. We were contacted by a customer who wanted some goods sent to her but said that the customs wouldn't let them in. We thought there must be something we could send her – they couldn't take exception to all our products – so we sent off a carefully chosen selection. There were no vibrators; only things like lingerie and his and hers garters and edible undies – all very tame really. We asked them to let us know which of the goods we could send and the reply came back that none of them would be allowed in: even a book called *All That Men Know About Women*, which contains nothing but blank pages, was rejected. Either the customs officers didn't even bother to look at what we sent, which I think is highly unlikely, or they took offence because they thought the items were too feminist. We circumvented the problem by sending the goods under plain cover and we have had no further difficulties.

As the company grew and grew and we had more and more people working hard to achieve their goals, it soon became clear that we had to offer incentives for the high-flyers or we would lose them. Taking the lead from other DSA members and Party Plan companies, we initially introduced a system whereby the women could win washing machines, dishwashers, televisions and other electrical goods. When a woman becomes a party organizer, she gets 30 per cent discount on everything she buys from us; once she has recruited six further organizers she can then be appointed as a unit organizer, receiving additional earnings on her team's sales; many girls earn more than £30,000 per year. We also run lots of competitions offering our sales force exotic holidays and other luxury prizes. Unit organizers have the further incentive of a company car, which starts as a white Ford Fiesta and is upgraded as set targets are achieved. Around a third of our unit organizers are proudly driving company cars which they have earned through their own hard work and determination.

We also decided to start holding an annual conference, which Party Plan companies used to boost morale and get everyone fired up to sell. Our first conference took place in 1984 at the Moat House Hotel, Elstree, Herts. I had held one on a very small scale the year before in the White Lion at Warlingham, and even though it was very informal everyone had a fantastic time and the whole event seemed to have a beneficial effect. Staff who knew about other Party

Plan companies told me that the Annual General Conference, or AGC, was always the big event of the year, with ladies nominated as 'best organizers' and so on. With their help and advice, I hired a room at Elstree on a very low budget. We had about 150 women sitting around the edge of the room at small round tables. In the early days the AGC was a one-day event and we offered the ladies a buffet lunch, but now it runs over a whole weekend. We started off inviting a few of the chief hostesses along as well, but numbers have grown so much that we have to restrict it to the unit organizers and staff. On that first occasion I remember wearing a red dress with little white triangular shapes on it. Every time I look at the photographs I think, 'Oh, God, what *did* I look like?'

The Annual Conference has always been regarded as the high point of the Ann Summers year and is a very important date on everyone's calendar. It is a chance to get all the unit organizers together and really motivate them. AGCs are always held at the beginning of the year: November is always our busiest month, with up to 8,000 parties a week, and January our worst. The organizers tend to switch off after Christmas, so we hold the AGC as early as possible in the New Year to get them back into the swing of things. There are now thousands of pounds worth of prizes for the top sales, the top recruiters, and many other categories.

We also offer prizes to the ladies who can come up with design suggestions for items of clothing or novelties that we then decide to manufacture. We call it the Design-a-Line competition and we receive many very workable ideas for sex aids or lingerie, accompanied by painstaking drawings. We allow the conference audience to vote on the ones they like the best, and the winner receives a cash prize for her initiative and the satisfaction of seeing her creation modelled at the next AGC and in the catalogue. This way the ladies dictate the product range themselves and can tell us exactly what it is they want.

There are also a great many men who think they have come up with the best possible design for a new sex aid. The thought and enthusiasm that have gone into some of the designs are astonishing. One man came up with the idea for a monitor to detect when a woman is faking an orgasm. It involved lots of wires and sticky pads – it must be a bit like one of those electrode slimming systems. The inventor was deadly serious: the monitor, he said, would be under the bed and the woman would be all wired up, and then, after love-making, the machine would give a reading which would tell the man whether she had had a genuine climax. Can you imagine any man thinking that any woman would agree to be wired up to such a machine in the first place? Yet this chap was convinced it would be a best seller and wanted me to endorse it.

Another man, a pensioner, wrote to me expressing sympathy for the plight of many single mothers today, forced into prostitution to make money or because they needed sex. He had women all wrong, but he thought he was doing us a favour by inventing a 'therapeutic centre for women':

> I have developed an idea which could give a lot of relief to females who no longer have a male partner or who may not wish to renew such associations. My problem is that I do not have the capital with which to get this service established. It is not something which the Department of Trade & Industry would assist with. I have tried to get people like Richard Branson interested . . . but the idea is not easy to sell.

He said he thought it could become 'a most lucrative addition' to our business and added: 'Once established, I cannot see any limits to which the service can extend on this planet.' Explaining his idea, he wrote:

> What is required is a centre where women can, in private, obtain sexual pleasure by self-applied artificial means. What is envisaged is a building, suitably located, where women can be shown into one of a dozen or so cubicles where they can, in

private, use the equipment operated by a slot meter, for as long as they choose. The equipment is an electrically operated machine fixed to the bottom of the bed from which a plastic rod protrudes and gives a thrusting action when the machine is in operation. An artificial penis would be attached to the rod.

It is believed that such a service would catch on quickly once it is viable and would be in demand by the following:

1. Widows
2. Spinsters
3. Divorcees
4. Separated females
5. Wives of:
   a) incapacitated husbands
   b) impotent husbands
   c) abusing husbands
   d) husbands lacking in libido

Ladies using this service can do so without fear of
   a) getting pregnant
   b) catching AIDS or other venereal disease
   c) being unfaithful

It is logical to assume that as soon as one establishment has proven its value they would need to be set up in very large numbers, not only throughout the country but abroad.

It could be a valuable export project. Once proven there should be no problem getting financial backing. A firm such as yours would also have no problems with regard to planning permission.

Poor man! You could hear the enthusiasm in his letter; he really believed he was on to a winner, but he has obviously never heard of vibrators! And can you imagine what the planning application to the local authority would say! Needless to say, that was one of the letters I file away into my speech file.

It is always men who send in the really wacky ideas. For them it is sheer fantasy and there is no practical basis to what they are suggesting. One of the funniest letters I received was from a chap who had a design for what he called a 'Love Seat':

It is basically a hammock supported from two anchorage points by ten adjustable straps, eight to support the woman's body and one for each of her feet. She is supported in a seated position three feet above the ground.

The benefits are as follows:

1.1. It allows the man to make love standing up, his most comfortable position, while the woman is cradled weightless where she can relax [as if she could!].

2.2. As love making is now relaxed it can be made to last for hours as it involves less physical effort for the man [anything for an easy life!].

3. It can reduce the chance of premature ejaculation.

He concluded: 'My company has been designing and making support harnesses for physiotherapy and surgical uses since 1985, albeit for the veterinary profession.'

After I received his letter I had visions of all these poor dogs and cats being placed in his contraption to test it out! I have had great mileage out of that letter, using it in my speeches and at conferences, and it never fails to raise a laugh.

Chapter Six
SILVA AND GOLD

VANESSA AND I were never particularly close as children, but that all changed during my early life with Tony. I can remember the very day that we became friends — she was about sixteen and I was twenty-three — and we have been virtually inseparable ever since. She came round to Biggin Hill with her boyfriend Paul and she and I went up to my bedroom for something and just started talking.

She told me how lonely and unhappy she was at home and, for the first time in my life, I told her how miserable I had been and we suddenly realized that, without knowing it, we had been going through much the same experiences and had a great deal in common. It was an emotional moment: we had found each other and I think our friendship was cemented from then on. It was a tremendous relief for us both.

Not that we didn't have our ups and downs, mainly caused by my awful clumsiness. On one celebrated occasion, Vanessa was at a photographic studio, modelling for the Christmas supplement. She was sitting having her hair and make-up done and I decided to help curl her hair with tongs — her hair is really fine and needs extra help. I picked up the tongs and rolled her hair around them right up to her scalp, and then I somehow managed to find the button that issued a jet of searing steam. Vanessa let out a yell: I had really burned her scalp! She was screaming and holding her head, and I was panicking and fussing and saying, 'Let me see, let me see.' As her big earrings were in the way, I said, 'Let me take these off.' I thought they were clip-ons and I yanked on them really hard – but they were for pierced ears. Poor Vanessa screamed even louder and her eyes filled with tears. I felt terrible. Needless to say, I was ushered out of the room, and after she had composed herself the shoot went very well – she is still, to my mind, one of the most beautiful models we have ever had. I think she must have got her good looks from my mother, who was stunning as a young woman and is still very attractive today.

I vividly remember an incident at our first AGC: Vanessa, aged seventeen, was modelling some of the lingerie. She was extremely nervous and things were very disorganized in those days. She was due to come out wearing this broderie anglaise number we had called Candy. It was a sort of body suit with white bloomers and an elasticated waist. It had a camisole top with little pink bows all the way down the front about as far as you could go, which only just tied it together, so that there was lots of bare flesh showing in between.

In the panic to change outfits quickly and get back on stage, Vanessa came out on to the catwalk with this outfit on back to front. I was devastated for her: as she walked out a few people started to suspect that it was on wrong, but when she turned around everyone knew because her buttocks were showing through the gaps in the pink bows and the bust part of the camisole top was flapping loose. We all have a good laugh about it now, but at the time she was absolutely mortified.

Nessy was partly responsible for the most embarrassing moment of *my* life. Her boyfriend Paul knew someone who was holding this swanky fancy dress party at a fort on an island in the Solent. I had just lost a lot of weight and felt absolutely fantastic and when I heard about this party I was over the moon: here was an opportunity to really go to town on my outfit and show off my new figure. I couldn't wait. Paul told us that the theme was black and white and decided to go as a jockey in a black-and-white silks; Vanessa was going as a French maid.

If I am going to do something I really like to do it better than anyone else, so I said to Tony, 'Let's really go to town and show them all!' He decided to go as one of the rock singers from the pop group Kiss, with all this weird hair and black-and-white make-up, and I decided to go as the devil's bride. I spent weeks preparing for it, going to all these punk rock shops and fancy dress places to buy the clothes and make-up. I wanted the sexiest outfit I could possibly get into and I didn't care who knew it.

In the end I have to say I looked outrageous. I wore a white cropped top with white lace sleeves, the shortest white mini-skirt you could ever imagine, with lace on top, and black stockings and suspenders. I was like something out of *The Rocky Horror Show*. I had dagger earrings and wild hair, out of which came little red horns. I also had a long red tail. Everything was done at our house – I did Tony's make-up too. It took hours but we looked great.

Six of us set off – the other couple were dressed as Dracula and a French maid – and people stared at us as we drove down to Hampshire. I know I looked completely over the top but I loved it. It was summer so it was still light when we arrived at the ferry point in Portsmouth: everyone was looking at us and pointing but we didn't care. The ferryman took us across and dropped us at the bottom of the stone steps to the fort. It was about eight o'clock and he told us he would be back to collect us at 1 a.m. With great excitement we climbed the steps to a courtyard and went through into a huge banqueting room.

Well, as we walked in, we looked at the other guests and they looked at us and we all froze. Everyone, but *everyone* in the room was in formal evening wear. The men were in black ties and dinner jackets and the women all in long black or white evening dresses. I didn't know where to put myself. I remember tugging at my little skirt to try and cover myself up. None of us even had coats to put on and, worst of all, the ferryman had gone so we were stuck there with all these stuffed shirts for at least five hours. The whole evening was a nightmare. We just had to act as normally as we could, and sit down to dinner with the others in their bow ties and jackets.

I tried very hard to see the funny side of it, but I couldn't. It was the most awful evening of my life.

The next day I just sat at home, stunned, going over the evening in my mind again and again. My aim had been to show off my new figure and boost my confidence and instead I had been publicly humiliated. It was typical of Paul to get the information wrong – I could have strangled him. If only I had known what the dress code really was I would have shown off my figure in a beautiful evening gown. The others were not nearly as upset as I was, but then if I had been dressed as a French maid and not the devil's bride, I would have coped too! I have never been to a fancy dress party since and I don't think I ever will. I just don't have the enthusiasm for it any more.

That story reminds me of something that happened to one of our customers. After she had bought an underwired basque, crotchless knickers, stockings and suspenders from her first Ann Summers party she decided to surprise her husband by meeting him from work dressed in sexy underwear and nothing else, under a raincoat. She put on her outfit, prepared a candlelit supper and drove to the station to meet him. To her dismay and embarrassment, he had invited his boss home for a drink. As she struggled back to the car in her high heels a gust of wind lifted her raincoat around her ears, revealing all to her open-mouthed husband, his boss and about fifty commuters pouring out of the station! She was absolutely mortified, her husband's boss made his excuses and left, and her husband was furious until he went to the office the next day and found that all his male colleagues had heard the story and were looking at him in a new, and rather envious light!

It was around this time that, without fully realizing it, I started to put myself under immense pressure at work. Indeed I had become a serious workaholic, staying in the office until ten o'clock at night before going home with my briefcase packed to the brim. I convinced myself that I had to empty that briefcase each night before I could start again the next morning. The weekends were the worst. I was very house-proud and tidy, and after cleaning the house I would start to work through my briefcase. People would drop round and ask us out and I would say that I couldn't possibly because I had too much work to do.

I lost sight of the difference between urgent and important. Of course everything is important, but you have to prioritize. I was paralysed by my own perfectionism, which was also having a dreadful effect on my marriage. Tony and I went to marriage guidance counselling and he told the counsellor about my compulsive list-making. I remember she laughed and said, 'I suppose you have a list telling you where all your lists are!'

A book called *The Complete Time Management System* helped me to break out of this obsessive cycle: it completely changed my life. I recognized instantly that I had a problem and by the time I had finished reading the book I knew I was a workaholic. Gradually I learned how to plan my work and work my plan.

This was in 1986 and I was twenty-six. I now have very high standards but I am no longer obsessively perfectionist. I addressed the problem and tamed it right down to a manageable level. I also learned the importance of delegating: if you don't delegate you stagnate. It took me a long time to accept the rule that, if there is someone who earns less than you do and who can do the same job competently, then you must delegate. Changing my life in this way released me from my own trap and allowed me to concentrate on doing the things I should be doing, not the things others should be doing. My confidence soared and I started to have a social life again. I found myself with a surge of ideas and a new interest in myself.

I had been so wrapped up in work that I hadn't taken proper care of myself before. Overweight and not particularly attractive, I had tried all sorts of diets – to no avail. Now I started going to aerobics classes four times a week and my whole appearance changed. I had my hair cut and styled professionally and started looking after myself. I lost 2 stone in weight, going from 9½ stone to 7½, which was much better for my 5 foot 2 inches.

Losing this weight changed my whole outlook: I felt I could wear more glamorous clothes and I started going out again. I regularly went clubbing with Vanessa – thanks to her my dress sense improved dramatically and I enjoyed the attention I was getting. I was always very flattered when people asked us which of us was the elder – there were seven years between us!

Unfortunately my marriage had suffered during the early days and Tony and I were gradually drifting apart. Ever the perfectionist, I was reluctant to admit defeat and that is why I sought help through professional counselling – which he agreed to go along to. There were three main problems as I saw it: firstly, Tony desperately wanted a family, but I knew that would trap me in the home; secondly, I was still very much a career girl – I was obsessed with running Ann Summers and making it bigger and better; and finally, I had suddenly found new confidence and energy and felt that Tony had not kept up with me.

There was one other reason why the marriage was shaky, but I am not sure that Tony would recognize it even now. Vanessa and I really had become very close – people used to say we were joined at the hip. I think he felt threatened by this, as Vanessa was taking up a lot of my time. We had a couple of rows about her: he didn't like to see us going off clubbing and having a good time.

Poor Tony, one minute he was married to this timid young girl who did everything he said and suddenly she had a mind of her own. First I had become engrossed in my work and plans for the future and then I was out clubbing. He did not know what to do, so he used to retreat to the comfortable macho atmosphere of Biggin Hill Flying Club and play cards with his mates. I hated every minute of the whole scene at the club, which was entirely male-dominated and sexist. When I meet a man, I know what he is thinking, but he doesn't say it. However, when Tony or a male friend would meet the same man, the man would say: 'What is she like? Does she wear all the kinky Ann Summers gear?' I was sure that was what they were saying up at the flying club.

In 1986 we moved to Chaldon, to an old school house with an air raid shelter in the garden, which was perfect for all the trimmings and materials that had previously been cluttering up our spare bedroom. It was all very quaint and we fell in love with it. I always thought it was funny that our road was called Willey Broom Lane. Tony really tried to win me round at that house: I remember he bought me two cats for Christmas. The cat of a friend of ours had given birth to kittens and Tony brought round the two black ones, a boy and a girl, so that I could choose one. Of course I couldn't choose between these two little black balls of fur so I had to have both. We called them Mowgli and Baloo and I adored them.

But no matter how much Tony spoilt me or how much in love with the house we were, the relationship was very stressed. He really did want a family and I think he felt a little uncomfortable with my success (he has changed a lot since then and is very proud of me). I was earning more than him and I think he hoped that D'Silva Designs and the new house would be a new start for him.

By this time he had left the management of the Ann Summers shops and opened a factory in which to place his outworkers. He proposed to borrow some money from the bank, because he knew my company couldn't afford to help him then, but my father said he would lend him the money. Dad always admired Tony's desire to succeed. The money enabled Tony to expand his business, which was ideal for us, as we were already struggling for suppliers who could keep pace with our growing demands. He was also used to dealing with our type of product – most of our manufacturers supplemented their income by making baby clothes as there was no money in lingerie in those days, and they simply had no idea of what was sexy.

The factory was in Thornton Heath. It was a single storey, red-brick building, very run down; it had previously been full of old machinery. Tony set up as a limited company and made me a director as well. A friend who ran a cleaning company cleaned it all up and we spent a whole weekend painting it. Tony was on a really tight budget and he couldn't afford anyone else to help him so, even though I had my own company to run, I just had to put on my jeans and get on with it.

He put an advert in the local paper and recruited people to come and work for him. The five or six outworkers were still employed during the overlapping period, but then the factory was up and running. He hates me to say this, but he reminds me now of Mike Baldwin in *Coronation Street*. His office is off to one side, with all the women working on their sewing machines in this big room, and he is in charge of them all. He has become a great asset to Ann Summers and still is, because he is so accommodating: he can quickly adapt to a different line and run us off fifty of something if we need it. He sells only to Ann Summers, although I have tried to persuade him not to put all his eggs in one basket. He produced a high percentage of our goods in the early days but now probably only accounts for 15 per cent of our range because we sell a lot of specialized corsetry and swimwear that he is simply not equipped to make. His operation is more geared to the playwear or funwear – the unstructured and skimpy garments with no bones, made of satin or soft lace.

Once Tony had his factory, our relationship seemed to improve for a while because I was no longer pressured by his insecurities, but I knew it was too late. My confidence had grown, my interest in him had diminished and we were growing apart in so many different ways. It all came to a head after I had been to Ireland on a business trip. That evening we were invited to dinner at a friend's flat in Sevenoaks. Even though I was living in this beautiful house and could afford a nice lifestyle, I really envied our hostess the little flat where she lived alone. I had never enjoyed that sort of independence as I had left home only to move in with Tony. He had always paid the bills and had never showed much interest in making a home, but all that was quite important to me.

After that dinner party I went to bed feeling incredibly unhappy. When I woke up the next morning I knew I could not live there any more. The house began to oppress me. Tony and I had an almighty row and I told him bluntly: 'I am so unhappy, I don't want to live with you any more. I want two weeks' break.' He was so upset he jumped in his car and drove off. I sat there, knowing I couldn't face him when he came back, so I stood up, repacked my case and drove to my father's house. Such was my loyalty to Tony that I had never let anyone suspect we had any problems. My perfectionist nature meant I had to hide what I saw as my failure. So my leaving came as a terrible shock to my family: they all thought we were the most happily married couple they knew.

I stayed at my father's for a night or two and then at hotels for a few weeks. Tony tried to persuade me to go back, but I knew I couldn't even though I was still very fond of him and it was painful for me to hurt him. Neither of us had an affair or anything like that: it was just over and we both found it very traumatic. We were married in 1980, separated in 1988 and divorced officially in 1990.

Tony's parents were devastated by the break-up. At first I shunned them – not deliberately for I love them dearly. I don't have lots and lots of friends; the special people in my life mean the world to me and Dorothy and Derek are two of them. They phoned me but I couldn't face talking to them – the whole thing was too upsetting. It was some time before I felt ready to see them again. When we eventually met they greeted me so warmly, as if I had been away for years.

I started looking for a flat – I had to get this flat thing out of my system – and after a while I found myself a brand-new two-bedroom flat in south Croydon for £90,000. I lived there for two years and loved every minute of it. It was a ground-floor flat in a red-brick purpose-built block, with its own driveway and parking. It was very comfortable, and beautifully decorated. I was in charge and in control and running my own finances. I finally had that independence I had been seeking ever since my childhood, when my mother had refused to let me out of her sight.

For some years Tony continued to try to get me back. He lived in this very stormy relationship for a while, but then he met Sally and they are very happy together. He has three children – a daughter of his own, and two stepchildren. After we split up he became a born-again Christian and I believe Sally is too and they seem very well suited. To my surprise I found it rather painful when he remarried. It wasn't that I had any desire to be back with him; he was just no longer my husband, but someone else's. He moved from the school house to a flat at Biggin Hill and eventually bought a house of his own.

I had seen my parents' marriage break up and remembered bitterly the unpleasantness, so I really wanted my divorce to be as friendly as possible. Tony and I had one or two tense moments – moments of desperation, I think – but we have never said a bad word about each other and are still very good friends and business colleagues.

I don't think I could ever have lived through my marriage break-up without Vanessa; she is still the most important person in my life. She works for me now but it was not always so. After Baston she went to a secretarial college, but she didn't get on with the headmaster so she left to work at one of the flying clubs at Biggin Hill. For quite some time she wanted to be an airline pilot or an air traffic controller – anything to do with flying, which was her new link with Dad. She was going to take flying lessons and do all sorts of things. She had always been a tomboy and liked to compete with the men she worked with. But everyone was always telling her how beautiful she was and how she would make a fantastic model. I don't think it was something that she particularly wanted, but she took their advice and joined a modelling agency. She got a few jobs, but she was very young and she didn't really know what she wanted to do.

She started working at Ann Summers casually between modelling assignments, doing menial jobs on the administrative side as I had done at first. She also did some modelling for us for a while and was featured on the front cover of one of our early catalogues. At this time she was living with Paul in Guildford; she stayed with him for six years, but after I split up with Tony she left him and I led her astray from that moment on. I think I opened up her eyes to the possibilities of life outside. For ages she was terrified of telling Mum about her split with Paul. When she came clean, it was all my fault, according to Mum, but she eventually calmed down and came to terms with Vanessa's decision.

Later on, when Vanessa and I started going out with two dancers, it was worse: as far as Mum's side of the family was concerned we were going out with a couple of strippers who had AIDS and God knows what else. Of course, they didn't have! For a while they had nothing to do with us, which only drew us even closer together: it was us against them, although Mum supported us throughout.

Vanessa's early days at Ann Summers were really just to earn a bit of pocket money, but she never left. She started in the post room and then became an operator on the Orderline – she was a general dogsbody really. In those days I don't think she understood what I was trying to achieve or who I was at all; I was still just her big sister, not her boss. She says the first time it registered with her was when she was in a position where she had to report directly to me. Even then we went through a bad patch when she would burst into my office unannounced, upset or angry about something, and flop down in a chair to let off steam. It took me some time to make her realize that this was my office, not my bedroom, and that she couldn't just burst in and behave like my little sister. My hints finally got through and she stopped doing it. Until then I don't think she had realized that I was a businesswoman.

I was also urging her to develop herself. I found myself wanting to solve all her problems, although all she wanted was sympathy and understanding. For a while she felt that I criticized everything she did or said. She was over-sensitive to criticism, I thought, so I sent her on a course to develop her interpersonal skills. I had always been fairly sceptical about these courses until I sent Vanessa. My theory was that you can't force people to learn: it's not like giving them a pill and expecting them to be cured. But although Vanessa was reluctant to go, she benefited from it enormously.

As I developed and grew as a woman and as a business success, Vanessa grew with me. Following in my footsteps I think it has been easier for her to accomplish things in her life. But she has also been a tremendous support to me in her quiet, unassuming way.

I am certain that she has never been at all envious of me. I think she is proud and impressed, but I think most of all she thinks: 'Thank God that is not me.' On several occasions she has been there to help calm my nerves when I am about to give a speech or make a presentation and I know she is thankful that it is me and not her going up to the podium. Mostly she wants to be someone I can rely on and trust implicitly – my right-hand woman.

Someone once asked Vanessa which of my qualities she most liked and she kindly said that I was very professional and a typical Cancerian – thoughtful of others. She said that one of the things she most admired was also something she found intensely annoying – my meticulousness. What was most infuriating, she said, was that I was always right: no matter how water-tight she believed an argument to be, I would always find its weak spot. My worst fault, according to Vanessa, is my obsession with being organized; everything is dictated by what she calls my 'plague of lists'. There was a time when my life was almost entirely ruled by lists. I used to have 100 different lists to cover everything; now I just have one long one! Vanessa still laughs when I give her my type-written multiple choice 'packing list' for holidays: everything that she could possibly need is listed, with little boxes to tick off as you go along. She also finds my dressing table very amusing: it has a drawer just for hair brushes, a drawer for hair grips — each type in a separate compartment, a stock drawer for spares of my cosmetics and hairsprays, and even a drawer full of miniature versions of everything to take in an overnight bag.

Vanessa and I have really lived our lives backwards. We left home having done nothing, found ourselves married or hitched, then ditched our partners, and now lead an almost single lifestyle. Since 1994 she has been my Marketing Manager at Ann Summers. Before that she was looking after several different departments and was sometimes a little out of her depth. She had a lot of responsibilities and more staff than she could cope with. I have concentrated her role down to something much more manageable and she has thrived on it. I gave her the job after making her undergo psychometric testing, which was very useful. She didn't see herself as an ideas person, although everyone else did, but she suddenly started to believe in herself. Previously we never had an official marketing function, but it suddenly became clear that we needed one and that, with further training, Vanessa was the obvious choice. I encouraged her to go for it and since her intense training programme she has never been more happy, positive or confident. This, in turn, has had a productive effect on her staff. She has eleven in all, and because of her new-found enthusiasm they are all doing much better too.

I think I understand Vanessa very well and I know how sensitive she is: I could only push her so far. A year ago she might have said she was happy to plod along where she was, but now she is forging ahead, looking to the future and possible promotion and realizing that she can achieve a lot more. She is very hard on herself and naturally feels she really has to earn her position on her own merits and not just because she is my sister. She has never given me any indication that she is as ambitious as I was, but then I kept a lot to myself. My guess is that she would like to work close to me in the future, but she wouldn't want to be out of her depth – she would only want a job if she was sure she could do it.

I have discouraged her from working with my father in those areas where the companies overlap because it was getting to be a problem for them both. Dad is not used to dealing with someone who is so emotional and who, as the boss's daughter and the boss's sister, is trying to prove herself. He was pretty poor at handling the situation and I often found myself intervening and mediating because he and I have a very high respect for each other.

Nessy would be the first to admit that I understand Dad better than she does. When I joined the company I always encouraged him to pick out my faults because I knew it was the only way I could learn, but he just couldn't understand why it didn't work the same way with Vanessa.

In other respects they get on very well. But I am probably the most influential person in Vanessa's life in every way and she is in mine, but away from the office our roles are almost reversed. At work, surrounded by business people, I am much more in control, and I can guide her through tricky situations. If she is feeling out of her depth I will always come to her rescue, as she has always come to mine.

Chapter Seven
SEXUAL XPERIENCE

PICTURE THE SCENE: a packed nightclub is pulsating with music and young people; it is late, everyone has had a few drinks and have been dancing the night away. Around midnight the disc jockey interrupts the music and tells the audience that something very special is about to happen.

The lights dim, the dance floor clears, and running into the spotlight come five gorgeous-looking dancers – men and women – dressed to kill. They launch straight into a raunchy dance routine and the audience goes wild. The pace quickens and the dancers start to peel off some of their outer layers of clothing: underneath they are wearing Ann Summers PVC garments which leave very little to the imagination.

As the audience start baying for more and reaching out towards the muscular bodies, Ann Summers organizers, wearing distinctive red sashes, move among them, handing out our latest catalogues. By the time the dance routine has come to a climax, with the men down to G-strings and the girls in skimpy underwear, hundreds of excited potential customers are flicking through the pages of the Erotica supplement and talking about getting together with a few friends for their first Ann Summers party.

It is a marketing dream to have such an unusual outlet for promoting the company; it was something that came about almost by accident and I was able to develop it into a successful enterprise.

The two dance troupes we have now – Xperience and Xcalibur – evolved from an embryo idea back in 1987. One of our organizers put together a fashion show using three girls and two guys she knew. She dressed them in Ann Summers products and put on a choreographed show in nightclubs, canvassing party bookings and recruits while the dancers were on the floor. She had some considerable success. After such positive initial feedback, she approached me to see if I would give them financial backing. I went along to one of the shows, which was held at Regals nightclub in Uxbridge, and was quite impressed. The show was not bad, although it needed some professional input.

I saw the potential and thought the scheme would be worth investing in. We re-choreographed the act and set it up properly as the Ann Summers Roadshow. Right from the start I told the dancers that they had to break even: if they ran at a loss I would have to scrap the idea. Using our new entertainment department, we approached nightclubs up and down the country to see if they would be interested in hiring our act. The arrangement was that the nightclub would pay about £700 to have the show as the highlight of their evening. The dancers would burst on to the dance floor and do their half-hour routine, starting off wearing something like dinner suits or trenchcoats and eventually stripping down to underwear. Initially it was really a fashion show and the guys were a prop for the girls, but in later shows they all became much more involved and, as tastes changed, so the show became raunchier and more professional.

At that time they worked at other jobs, doing their show in the evenings to earn a bit of extra money. Now they are all professional dancers; two remain from the original line-up. They travel all over the country in our own tour buses, averaging about four shows a week.

The Ann Summers Roadshow really started to take off. All the local organizers would be invited to attend shows in their area and would hand out the catalogues and try to get bookings. We were getting between twenty and a hundred bookings from each performance. It was the first time we had ever actively recruited the public and, of course, the shows attracted media publicity.

The original line-up was Jodie Nurton, a housewife and mother of two, two models called Lara and Lisa, an electrician called Stuart Turner and another man called Nile. Jodie was great – very bright and bubbly – and was in the show for seven years. Lara had to leave when she broke her leg and when Nile left, he was replaced by Sandra Evans's son, Steve (Sandra was the lady who came to the job interview thinking we sold children's clothes). The boys originally became involved only because they were working part-time as doormen; the club owners suggested they should escort the female dancers through the crowds to the dance floor so that they didn't get molested. After a while Jodie offered the boys some extra cash if they would wear boxer shorts, and they eventually became an integral part of the act.

By 1988 they had been renamed the Ann Summers Xperience and were not only touring Britain but travelling abroad. I was delighted with their success and in November decided to go and see one of their performances in Ireland. They went down extremely well: I don't think the Irish had ever seen anything like them. That was the night I first started chatting to Stuart, one of the dancers. We really hit it off, and it was after that trip that I decided to leave Tony. I was very impressed by Stuart. I found him very confident and decisive and he also looked great and took very good care of his body, which, by then, was important to me.

He was also intellectually stimulating, something I respect more and more as I grow older. I don't want to be either dominated or dominating in a relationship. I want it to be on equal terms. A little while later I went to see some more shows – sometimes with Vanessa and sometimes with Sandra. I had more time on my hands anyway and, after all, it *was* business. I started seeing more and more of Stuart and in January 1989 our friendship developed into a relationship.

Stuart made the first move, as I am a bit old-fashioned. I was very attracted to him but, in all honesty, I didn't think it would last. His lifestyle was quite different to mine. However, like Tony, he was extremely hard-working – something I respect in a partner.

Although Stuart's background was not at all like mine, I found him very interesting. He impressed me: he had a lot of confidence and was proud of the way he looked, working out regularly in the gym. He was so different to Tony. I think Stuart would say that I was not what he expected either: he had imagined someone rather crass and full of herself, but we liked each other immediately.

He lived at West Drayton, near Heathrow Airport, and worked as an electrician on a building site. What with his shows and my work schedule, we didn't see that much of each other at first. When we *did* get together it was always great fun. He was witty and had a great sense of humour; his personality was very outgoing and he could chat easily to strangers. He certainly didn't want to be on a building site all his life, so I told him I thought he would make a great salesman. That is when my respect for him grew enormously: there he was with a trade and a regular income and a mortgage to pay, but I had only to mention this idea to him and he became determined to be a salesman for a reputable company. He went to some sales agencies but was turned down because he had no experience. Then an opportunity came up for a job with Canon – based in the City which he had a very high regard for. We had decided to go to Tenerife for a week's holiday and he applied for the job just before we went. They made an appointment for after the holiday and he was over the moon: once he had his foot in the door, he was convinced he could persuade them to take him on.

But when we got back the agency told Stuart that the job had been filled while he was away. I was very sorry for him; he had bought a suit specially for the interview and was so sure of the job. Then, all of a sudden, he stood up and put his suit on. I asked him what he was doing. He said he was going to go along for the interview anyway and pretend he didn't know that the job had gone; he reckoned that he still had a chance. I was very impressed. Off he went and underwent psychometric testing and gave them all the old flannel. The next day they rang him up and said he had the job. I don't think they had actually taken on anyone else but they must have liked his enthusiasm and assertiveness: he had exactly the right personality and drive for a job in the City.

When Stuart left the building site he was probably earning around £20,000 a year and he had to drop to £6,000 with no commission during his nine-month training period. It was a big risk for someone with a mortgage, but he took it. For a year he worked in the City and then he was transferred to Reigate. Now he is a senior salesman – often top in his region – with a nice company car, and is earning far more than he could ever have dreamed of as an electrician. I really admire his achievement.

I think Stuart recognizes that I gave him the security and the inspiration to go for it when many people would have played safe. I also gave him support and encouragement during his first three months and tried to be as flexible as I could with my time. However, it was his determination that got him the job in the first place.

He is still one of the most popular dancers in the Ann Summers troupe, but I rarely go to see him performing – maybe twice a year. It is not as glamorous as people may think, and because I am in charge of Ann Summers it is not a relaxing situation for me.

In the early days we lived some distance from each other, but this was not a problem because we both needed our space. I thought then, and still do, that maintaining that space between two people keeps a relationship alive. I do love him and we get on very well, but I think I feel the same way about marriage as I do about children – why change things if you are happy? When you have been married once there doesn't seem to be that urgent need to marry a second time. Stuart now lives in a flat in Caterham Valley – quite close to where I eventually moved after I sold my flat (for £10,000 less than I paid for it!). By that time I had the independence thing out of my system and I didn't like the restrictions of a flat – nosy neighbours, no garden and no privacy. The time was right and I wanted a house, so I bought a very nice four-bedroom detached house in Caterham-on-the-Hill. It was new when I bought it. The builder had gone bankrupt so it had no interior and I brought my own builder in and finished it off the way I wanted, which was great fun. It has a real Swedish feel to it, with lots of wood throughout, and I love it.

We formed another dance group, Xcalibur, in February 1993, when the Chippendales were all the rage in the UK (I always thought they were far too slushy). Xperience were doing very well, so I thought it might be a good time to set up an all-male show as well to attract all-female audiences.

It was not as easy as I had thought to find five men who looked good, danced and were prepared to take their clothes off. My first thought was to find an existing dance group, pick out the best dancers and train them up properly. There was a group called Fourplay, run by the lead dancer Tim Kent, who was a *Sun* page seven fella and also one of the 'Dream Men' featured in our male pin-up calendar. There are very few male glamour models but the ones I know are utterly charming and very good at their own PR – they always include you on their Christmas card list!

We wanted to get the group ready in time to spring a surprise at our Annual Conference, but the deal fell through: the dancers pulled out, we were messed around and I was back to square one. However, Tim Kent had told other models in the industry what we were doing and so the word spread. I didn't think male models would really be interested; they earned around £300 a day for a fashion shoot, so why do a dance routine three nights a week for £90 a night?

Anyway, one day Vanessa and I were in a wine bar in Croydon and this model called Steve Golding was there. He is 6 feet 2 inches, gorgeous, blond, tanned – the works. We started talking and all of a sudden he seemed very interested. He said there was a recession in modelling like everything else, and he could do with the extra income. Stuart was also interested in moving from Xperience to Xcalibur, so we set up a meeting and Steve turned up at the offices with five gorgeous hunks. You can imagine what the girls in the offices thought about that – they kept finding excuses to come and have a good look.

The original line-up was Steve Golding, John Huntley, Glen Davies, Kevin Cardine, Dave Ingram and Paul Kevin (Stuart didn't join until later). Vanessa held the meeting and persuaded them all to sign up. They had a gruelling rehearsal schedule as the next Annual Conference was looming. We hired a choreographer who said that initially they were a nightmare to train. He had to instil some discipline into them and he was tearing his hair out in the early days because they would arrive late and forget their kit and there seemed to be problem after problem.

I remember I went to one of the dress rehearsals: Xperience did their routine first and were absolutely spot on; then the boys came on and they were terrible. Having seen the professionalism of Xperience I think they were really embarrassed. However, in the end they went down an absolute storm at the Annual Conference and were completely overwhelmed by the audience response.

A few minor problems aside, they have been a riproaring success ever since. The girls in the nightclubs scream at them to get their clothes off. Nowadays the dancers are very careful not to get too close to the audience – several of them have suffered quite serious scratches and bruising from the more boisterous girls; quite a few have had their underwear literally ripped off in the excitement! The men do strip down to G-strings and go through some pretty explicit motions with volunteers from the audience, but all in all, it is good clean fun and they do nothing that would embarrass the Party Plan party-goers!

It is not only the women in the audience who cause problems. On one occasion, when Stuart was still with Xperience, he was half-naked in bondage gear – boots, collar, thong and handcuffs – and was waiting in the crowd to run on to the dance floor and join the girls at the appropriate moment. All of a sudden a fight erupted near by. The bouncers moved in very quickly, opened a rear fire exit and pushed the group of trouble-makers outside, where the fight continued. In all the confusion poor Stuart was also pushed outside. It was a freezing cold night, and there he was, standing there in his gear and very little else, banging on the door trying to get back in. No one heard him, so he had to run all the way round to the front door and persuade the doormen there to let him in. He rushed down to the dance floor, still shivering, and all the girls could say was: 'Where the hell were you?'

Having the dancers on board has been great fun. As Managing Director I have offered many times to line them up in my office naked and properly examine their credentials, but they have always refused (apart from Stuart, of course!). Despite what they do they are surprisingly embarrassed when they have to emerge from the changing area at costume fittings. Some of their most popular outfits are dungarees (for their car wash routine, which features sponges soaked in soapy water – that really gets the ladies going!), US military uniforms, and gangster costumes in pink, yellow and blue. It is one of my jobs to check that the costumes fit perfectly. As I say to the hundreds who volunteer, it is a tough job, but I am prepared selflessly to undertake it myself!

Neither troupe is a threat to the other: they share the jobs out. Xperience do a lot of work at Butlins' adult weekends, which have been going for some years. They are only one of many acts. When they are not at Butlins, they are performing four or five nights a week, which is very demanding.

Indeed, the job is so exhausting that it nearly cost Stuart his life a few years back. He was driving the minibus, full of equipment, back to the office one night and fell asleep at the wheel. The van went off the motorway, hit a crash barrier and then a tree and the indicator stick went straight into Stuart's face. The police rang me at home that night and I rushed to the hospital, took one look at his face (which was covered in blood), and promptly fainted! They put me on the bed next to his to come round! Stuart, fortunately, made a full recovery. A few days later we had a rather strange phonecall from the police, who told us that they had recovered all the thongs, bondage wear and whips that had been strewn across the motorway, but asked if we would mind if they kept them. I imagine their policemen's balls were never the same again.

Both groups are very successful all over Europe and outshine the competition by miles – partly because we put a lot of money into their training and costumes. As long as they don't make a loss, we consider it money well spent; generally they are just in profit. Many of their benefits are hidden (unlike their assets!), and it is difficult to quantify the ways in which they help with things like car presentations to organizers and the launch of new catalogues.

Vanessa is in charge of them (lucky girl) and is ably supported by Julie Harris, my Sales Director. Julie joined us in the 1980s after working as a sales manager of three boutiques in Gillingham, Kent. She is married to a policeman and left her job to start a family. When her two children were quite small, she wanted to return to work and decided to join Ann Summers as a Party Plan organizer. I think she had hosted a couple of parties and thought it would be fun. At this stage I already had three executive regional managers; Sandra Evans was one and she informed me that there was a lady in her team who was full of fun and very good. I had met Julie once or twice and I was impressed, so I agreed that Sandra should promote her to Area Manager. Shortly after that I needed to recruit another executive regional manager because I had to let one of the others go. I decided that it had to be Julie, despite the fact that she was so new. Some people thought the job should have gone to someone who had been there longer, but I have always believed that you employ the best person for the job, not just the one who has been there longest.

It was not long before I decided I needed a national sales executive – someone between me and the regional executives. Julie was too new and I didn't feel that the others were right. This was October 1991, and I was approached by a man called Peter Cartwright, a young, vivacious and dynamic executive who had just left Pippa Dee. I had met him a few times before at DSA conferences, and I agreed to interview him. Impressed by his enthusiasm and drive, I appointed him European Sales Executive and continued dealing with the executive regional managers myself.

Peter worked for us for about six months and then he was headhunted to be Managing Director of Dorling Kindersley, Party Plan publishers, which was a fabulous opportunity for him; I had no choice but to let him go. Once again I decided that I really needed someone between myself and the execs and I was looking around for another Peter Cartwright. All the execs were feeling a little unsettled at this time because they did not know who was going to be brought in and, frankly, neither did I.

One night in January 1992 Julie and I were working late after a board meeting. I had come to know Julie very well and she and I were sitting surrounded by curling sandwiches and coffee cups and we just started talking about the business in general. We talked and talked for ages, and it suddenly dawned on me that here was the very person I needed, sitting right in front of me. I hadn't even considered Julie before because she was one of the executives and part of the team. I didn't tell her there and then; I like to mull things over for a day and a night if I can. I called her in to see me the next day and gave her the offer of promotion. She just sat there and looked at me, completely stunned.

The first thing she said was: 'I can't possibly do that, I don't speak German,' which was not the reaction I expected – it really threw me. She had assumed I was looking for a copy of Peter and knew that she wasn't in the least like him. She thought that she lacked dynamism and experience, but I told her I had every confidence in her and that she would develop her own style, which would be just as good as Peter's – and, of course, I was right.

She left the room to think about it. I couldn't believe it: I had just offered her a fantastic opportunity and she had reacted in this way; but a couple of hours later she came back to see me and she was a totally different person – she was almost leaping around the room with delight. Goodness alone knows why she doubted herself; people respect her because you know exactly where you stand with her and she is wonderfully motivating and reassuring. Sandra Evans was thrilled about her protégée's promotion.

Julie has had a number of very funny experiences at official police functions. On one occasion she was sitting at a dinner table with her husband's chief inspector and his wife and a few others when a lady across the table recognized her and, in front of everyone, came out with: 'Oh by the way, one of those love balls you sold me [little balls you wear in your knickers to help the day go more smoothly!] has cracked.' Julie told me there was a stony silence around the table as she stumbled for a reply, only to be saved by the chief inspector's wife saying: 'Oh yes, those – they are jolly good, aren't they?'

Another time, she was at the check-out in Tesco's and couldn't find her cheque book. Without thinking, she turned out the contents of her rather large handbag and rummaged through it. When she looked up, the people in the queue behind her were looking at her with their mouths open and the check-out girl was signalling to her friend on the next aisle to come over and have a look, for there, lying in all its glory on the conveyor belt, was a huge vibrator, the Caesar, complete with warts and knobbly bits. Julie just sighed, picked it up and put it back in her bag, breaking the silence by asking if she could pay now. She says she has had funny looks in Tesco's ever since.

Julie's two children are now twelve and thirteen. She is the perfect mother and wife and is absolutely devoted to her family. She is very busy at work and spends quite a few nights away from home, but she is constantly making it up to her children, taking them cycling and swimming and camping, and very rarely missing a school function. As I see it, she has the balance absolutely right, but it wasn't always so. Some years ago she came in from work one night and her husband gave her a sticky label which said MUMMY, so that her children would know who she was. That really made her sit up and think, and since then she has made sure that she spends more time with them.

Julie and I have a very special relationship: we have been through a lot together. She is impulsive in her approach to things and I am the opposite, so we complement each other very well. I rely on her and we have become very close. I don't socialize with her because we don't need to as we spend so much time together at the office, but I know that I can talk to her about anything. She has supported me through a lot of difficulties. Everyone needs that one person they can lean on and who is there for them. She is that for me.

At the 1992 AGC Julie persuaded me to do something I have never done before – something that was completely out of character for me. We are always looking to make each conference better than the one before and that year we had decided the theme would be 'Let's Work Together'. As usual, the dancers were scheduled to perform the grand opening because it creates such an impact with the ladies. We plan the event nine months in advance and I remember saying at the first committee meeting that this year we needed to do something really different when the dancers came on.

Someone said jokingly: 'Wouldn't it be great if Jacqueline did a dance routine with the male dancers?' and we all laughed, including me. It was Julie, of course, who piped up: 'Yes, that's a brilliant idea!' I said, 'You can't be serious!' and she looked at me the way she does when she knows I can be persuaded. Julie said that the organizers would absolutely love it – she knows I am a soft touch when it comes to 'my girls'. I thought: Why not go for it?

It is all very well agreeing to something that is nine long months away, but the time slipped away alarmingly quickly. Vanessa, who organizes the choreographer, sat down with me and we agreed that the dance routine had to have impact and surprise. Because of my busy schedule, the rehearsals took place on Sundays at the Dance Attic in Fulham. I was to dance with five of the guys - three from Xcalibur and two from Xperience, including Stuart. While I was looking forward to it in a way, I was also very apprehensive: here were these guys who (apart from Stuart, of course), were used to seeing their Managing Director in a suit, and all of a sudden the roles were being reversed and I was having to learn their job. I felt rather self-conscious in this role reversal.

Paul Domain, the choreographer, was brilliant and very patient. I told him I was so clumsy that I couldn't even get the steps right in my aerobics class. He spent the first couple of sessions with me on my own to build my confidence and we worked out a routine that I could cope with. I learned how to count the beats and when to do my steps. When the guys joined in they gave me loads of encouragement; they are used to doling out flattery to women and they helped me a lot.

I was to do a routine with each of them and at the end they had to lift me up above their heads, to the fullest stretch of their arms; being so short, I found it frightening being that high up. The skill was not getting up there; it was staying up there. During rehearsals I fell off dozens of times, and the guys ended up with their hands in all sorts of unusual places, but we all had a laugh about it!

When the big day arrived I had a minor attack of stage fright. I wanted it to be perfect. I knew the audience would be astounded, but if it went wrong it could all backfire. The boys were nervous too: Paul had told them that if I made a mistake, they were to follow me so that it wouldn't look wrong to the audience.

The audience cheered as the guys ran out on to the dance floor. While they did their routine I stood in the wings, with the choreographer's assistant counting me in. Finally they stood in a diagonal line across the stage and I came on, strutting past them in a smart black trouser suit. There was this delayed reaction from the audience and then a gasp as people started to realize that it really was who they thought it was up there on the stage. Then there was this tumultuous applause which really encouraged me. The boys had talked about the adrenaline rush you get doing the routine for real in front of an audience, and now I knew what they meant.

My routine went smoothly and then it came to the lift. What I hadn't allowed for was that boost of adrenaline: I rushed at the boys and they in turn launched me up into the air ten times faster than we had ever done in rehearsals. Watching the video, I can see the tension on my face at this point. However, I managed to stay up and the applause that greeted us was fantastic.

I had a radio mike strapped to my body during the routine because immediately afterwards I had to give my opening speech. Fortunately everyone was still clapping as I stood there, trying to regain my composure. I said something like: 'I can't believe I just did that,' and they all clapped even more. I think it meant a lot to them that the MD had done something so unusual and different. When I had caught my breath I told them that because the conference theme this year was 'Let's Work Together', Julie had had the idea of me doing the routine to bring the point home. I added, half-jokingly and completely off the cuff, that next year I would make Julie do a solo tap-dancing routine and they all roared with laughter at the idea. I did eventually get my own back on Julie, as you will discover.

For weeks after I was being congratulated on the routine, and people told me how much it had meant to them. It was great fun.

Chapter Eight
THE MIDAS TOUCH

A**S ANN SUMMERS** became more and more successful and started to generate large amounts of cash, I was able to plan for the future and reinvest money in what was fast becoming a very respectable concern. We were suddenly in a position to acquire companies that were manufacturing items that we needed in large quantities.

The money coming into the Gold Group of companies also released my father and Ralph from financial constraints and enabled them to expand and develop their own concerns. My father says that it was around this time that he fully realized I was achieving my potential. He said that, with a third Gold in charge, it felt like the Three Musketeers all over again, only this time even bigger and better.

There were other changes afoot that influenced our decisions: the Government introduced new sex licensing laws, which I personally think was a good idea. The plan was to clamp down on the undesirable seedy shops, bars and clubs sprouting up all over Soho by introducing a licence which you had to apply and pay for. There was no set fee or banding, like the rates system; the individual councils set their own fees, which could and did range from £500 to £20,000.

We were dealing mainly with Westminster and Camden councils and you had to send the money in together with your application for a shop. If you didn't get the licence you didn't get your money back and that was that. The system was actually very unfair, although it did weed out the cheaply run, tackier shops who didn't even apply because they could not afford the fee. We struggled a little at the outset because we lost some licences coupled with a concious decision to reduce shops in certain areas we closed down seven of our twelve shops.

Fortunately this coincided with our plan to bring the shops more into line with the idea behind Party Plan. We found that we didn't necessarily need licensed shops — which are anyway supposed to carry no more than 10 per cent of the overall range of sex aids and books. This is actually not a written law, it is an understanding. Now only two of our shops are licensed — the others are not officially sex shops. Queensway carries only a small range of vibrators, for which you don't need a licence. Our flagship Charing Cross Road site is licensed and has a very large adult section at the back. The shop has been completely refurbished: you walk in to be greeted by an understated swirling green effect (very female friendly). There are no large empty expanses — just glass partitions and rails which encourage you to walk around. With its soft lighting and background music it has a much more comfortable atmosphere than the old-style shops. The adult centre at the back is signposted and completely sectioned off, so you don't have to go in if you don't want to. This is where you will find the more risqué bondage, rubber and PVC wear, and the videos (of which, incidentally, Party Plan only sells about three).

In the old days some of the shops — like the warehouse — were occasionally raided by the police, but only the magazines were confiscated. The publishers, the printers, the wholesalers and even the newsagents would also be raided — a financial burden which had to be borne by Gold Star. The raids were serious but they never threatened to put the company out of business because they were costed into the budget.

While Ann Summers was growing, so was the Gold Group, which now has twenty companies under its wing and a turnover in excess of £100 million. In addition to the publishing and distribution, the group is involved in textile printing, property, telephone dating and the publication of maps and tourist guides.

Before we took it over in 1987, Gossip, our textile printers in Kent, used to operate out of no more than a little shack, printing all our slogan T-shirts and nightshirts. We sell items like Louisa, a playsuit with a large hand imprint on the breast and buttock region, a maternity nightshirt with LET ME OUT written on it, and a cheeky T-shirt called Bone Love printed with fluorescent skeletons in different sexual positions. This range is extremely popular and formed a large proportion of our sales. We were quite dependent on Gossip, and were horrified to learn that they were in financial difficulty.

Fortunately they were renting premises from one of our other suppliers, so we took on the rent and the staff salaries and paid all the bills. We moved cautiously at first, in case the owner returned, but he never showed up so we set up the company anew, giving it a different name and moving it to an industrial estate in Maidstone. The company now exists in its own right. It is very successful and Simon is still there as our manager. They sell to us, of course, but they also produce T-shirts as incentives for companies like Ford, who may want specific designs printed up for special promotional events.

Also in 1987 my father and Ralph became 50 per cent owners of the *Sport* Group of newspapers, after striking a deal with David Sullivan. Long before the Ann Summers success, when magazine publishing was the major part of the business, David Sullivan ran a company called Conegate. This was one of Gold Star's main competitors, but funnily enough we distributed some of its magazines.

The relationship between Sullivan and the Gold brothers was initially strained; at first they would only ever meet on neutral ground, such as a hotel, but eventually they decided to go into partnership to set up the *Sport*. Sullivan was looking for financial support and he knew that Dad and Ralph could help. The *Daily* and

Sunday Sport were recently valued in excess of £50 million, so their investment paid off.

The Golds and Sullivan now get on very well and have become close friends. Sunday Sport newspapers also owns 83 per cent of Birmingham City Football Club. Dad and Ralph have become totally absorbed in the club; they go to watch every match, home and away, and have invested money in the new stadium. Football is their passion.

I have never been involved in the *Sport* and have not advertised Ann Summers in the newspaper because it was largely aimed at men, not women, and did not fit in with our image.

In October 1987 the Gold Group acquired Broglia Press in Bournemouth, another company in financial difficulty. Although we used two other printers, the whole group relied on Broglia very heavily – Gold Star for the magazines and Ann Summers for the books and stationery. We bought them out and they now publish all the Ann Summers catalogues and leaflets, as well as literature for a number of commercial companies from British Gas to Barclays Bank. They recently invested several million pounds in the latest state-of-the-art printing machinery from Germany.

All the companies within the group have to be competitive. They know that they don't get any special favours: if they don't give me a good price, I will take my business elsewhere. They also know that they cannot just survive on Ann Summers. The first takeover I personally supervised was the Lovelace deal. I quickly learned that you have to move immediately and not allow the deal to stretch out, expecting the organizers to wait while you sort out the final details – that way you end up losing and I don't like losing.

There are many different management styles and philosophies within the group. My style is more persuasive; Gold Star is much more aggressive, but as we work together I think my persuasiveness is rubbing off. I am much more of a team player and am more democratic in my approach. In some companies the senior people feel threatened by quality people coming up through the ranks, but

I enjoy giving my staff credit for ideas and this in turn boosts their confidence.

Ann Summers is a unique operation: it offers housewives and mothers, often tied to the home, a chance to escape. They can get together with a group of friends for a drink and something to eat, and have fun being shocked and titillated. If they wanted to be bored they would go to a party selling plastic freezer boxes, but they don't: they dress up and they go to an Ann Summers party to play games like a naughty version of Pin the Tail on the Donkey, and they get to see, hold and touch things normally only available in sex shops. The atmosphere is like a hen night; we often get three generations at our parties – grandmothers, daughters and grand-daughters – and they all have tremendous fun.

When they eventually go home, having ordered a vibrator or a sexy piece of underwear, they feel excited, desirable and inspired. Many tell me that their husbands find they are really in the mood when they come home from parties! They can have that fun on a regular basis, in their own time, earning not just a bit of extra cash for Christmas, but money that often puts their husbands' wage packets to shame. With such small overheads, they are on to a winner.

The starter kit is rented for £2.50 a week initially until they have achieved certain targets, when it becomes their property and then they are up and running. Friends and neighbours are per-suaded to be hostesses for 10 per cent of the party takings, plus an exclusive item of lingerie and further incentives dependent upon party sales. The organizers meet their customers directly, in the comfort and privacy of a friend's living room. This all-female, adult environment – all men are strictly banned and no party member must be under eighteen years of age – provides the stimu-lus to buy: 97 per cent of party-goers come away having ordered something, and the average spend is between £20 and £22.

Ann Summers is made up of remarkable women, from the

newest recruits to the highest achievers, and we pride ourselves on the opportunities we offer them. They start by holding their own parties, then someone at one of those parties asks to join, and so it goes on from there. From tiny acorns do mighty oaks grow and, like me, many women have gone from strength to strength. They begin rather nervously — their starter kits hidden under the stairs — but go on to become hugely successful unit organizers, with dozens of ladies under them. The prizes they win, the awards they pick up at the Annual Conferences, and the prestige they gain gives these housewives and mothers the confidence and motivation to achieve career success and financial independence in a way that many of them never dreamed of.

There are many, many women whom I have watched come up through the ranks in this way. I hope they know they all have my greatest admiration and support. But there is one particular woman whom I — and women throughout the company — will always remember: Loretta Leese. She was the ideal Ann Summers organizer, completely dedicated to the company and her team of ladies, and her energy and enthusiasm inspired so many others. She showed such courage in the face of terminal illness, to which she sadly succumbed after four years. It started with breast cancer, which she successfully fought after a mastectomy, but which then became secondary.

In late 1991 she was told she only had two months to live, but she still managed to attend the Annual Conference even though she was in a wheelchair. We gave her a special Award of Excellence for her courage. When she made it up to the stage on her crutches to receive it, Julie and I just burst into tears.

I also remember going to her area meeting (I try to go to one a month), and there she was, even though she was so ill. She told me that sometimes her organizers cancelled parties at the last minute and asked her to arrange someone to cover because they had a headache ('They just don't know how lucky they are,' she commented). On one occasion, her organizers told me, she even checked herself out of her hospice one night to hold a party rather than let her customers down. Ann Summers was her life – I think that was what kept her alive for so long against all the odds. She had the support of her wonderful husband, Alan, who gave up his job to look after her in the final years.

She died in December 1994. She was still in her thirties and had young children. I went to her funeral in Derby: the church was packed and there were scores of Ann Summers apple wreaths for her to show the love and support she had from us all. I didn't know what to do to help in those circumstances, but as a small gesture I asked Alan to keep her company car. No matter how many ladies you have, and I currently have 7,500, they are all very important to you.

In December 1990 I set up a special conference for the top fifty achievers – the Graduates Guild (of which Loretta was a member). The idea came from delegates at the DSA conferences who said that a club for the elite few helped to keep the targets up. Originally I made it the top 200 ladies, but reduced it after a while because 200 just wasn't elite enough. The club offers certain benefits, but, more important, it confers a great deal of prestige. They wear badges to which they can add 'achievement bars' for being the top recruiter, best in sales and so on. These bars eventually form long chains, like golden ladders, which hang down from the badge and are looped back up again. Every link signifies a woman's success in the company and they are worn with tremendous pride.

The benefits include special catalogue previews, business gifts, their own VIP reception at the Annual Conference, and competitions where up to ten women can win exotic holidays with their partners. I know from speaking to organizers at the lower levels that they dream of making it to the Graduates Guild one day.

We all need motivating and I try to spend time recognizing other people's achievements. I want them to know that I am aware if they have done something particularly good. The trouble about getting to the top, though, is that there is no one above you to do the same for you. I don't need to be constantly patted on the back, fortunately, and I am motivated by the successes and enthusiasm of others. My wonderful PA, Carol Morris, is good at looking after me. She joined me in 1993 and tells me I am stuck with her now until she retires. I was very interested to hear how she came to work with me.

One day she saw me being interviewed on *UK Living* with Jane Irving, and was apparently so impressed that she told her husband that night that she would love to work for someone like me. She had been looking for a new job for a while and, two weeks later, she spotted a small box ad in the *Croydon Advertiser* for a PA/secretary. She telephoned the agency and asked which company it was. They were rather cagey at first and warned her that she might not approve. When they eventually told her she badgered them for days to get her an interview. I liked her immediately and we get on famously. Now that her two children have grown up, she concentrates all her energy on me, and I don't know what I would do without her.

I love to see other people's success but I am also stimulated by failures and problems which present a new challenge. We faced a problem with the parties: if a party organizer was prevented from attending a party (she might be delayed, or taken ill, or had a breakdown – or forgotten or moved without passing on the details of the party) there was a danger of disappointing a valued hostess, who had prepared food and drink for, say, fifteen friends and was anticipating a 'naughty but nice' evening.

In response to this, in August 1991 we set up a night coverage service – effectively a sort of head office emergency breakdown number: if the organizer doesn't arrive for a party, the hostess can call in and get a replacement organizer sent to her. The scheme was thought up and is now run by Yvonne Fairman. When she gets a call, she rings round everyone in that area to find a stand-in. Some parties emerge from such a crisis to become a tremendous success: by the time the organizer arrives everyone is so pleased to see her that they spend lots of money and the party goes really well. If the service salvages a situation like that even once a week, then it is worth it.

In February 1992 we were due to have our usual Annual Conference; it was also our tenth anniversary so we knew we had to do something special. We had been holding it at the Birmingham Metropole every year because it was so central for everyone, but this time we decided to go to the Grand Hotel in Jersey. I even took my mum and her friend along, which was a special treat for me and I know she really enjoyed it. We just took the whole hotel over: we had so much equipment to set up that our huge lorry had to have a police escort from the ferry to the hotel. We were expecting over 400 ladies and Matthew Kelly was the compère. He was our first real celebrity and he was so brilliant we had him two years running. All the celebrities love our conferences; they say they have never seen anything like it, what with the live floor shows, the fashion shows and the cutting of the apple cake. The team spirit is amazing, and at the awards ceremony (depending on the previous years' achievements, organizers can win videos, holidays or cars) all the women jump up and down and scream and shout with delight. It is not like any ordinary conference. The whole event costs about £250,000 each year, but it is money well spent as it motivates and hypes everyone up for the year ahead. We employ an outside company to video the AGCs and then sell it to our organizers at a fraction of the cost, as a memento of the big event.

The theme of this particular conference was based on the pop song 'The Only Way Is Up' – we choose a different hit each year and every time the ladies hear it on the radio afterwards, they think of Ann Summers and the conference theme.

I arrived on the Tuesday with my team and the ladies were due to arrive on the Saturday morning in time for a buffet lunch. We had chartered planes to make sure everyone arrived on time, but there was absolute panic because I hadn't taken into account the

Channel Island fog. There were all sorts of problems and delays and we sat in tense groups around the hotel, waiting for the last group of ladies to arrive. They came in to a huge cheer and, two hours later, the conference was underway.

We always start with the dancers, usually the ever popular Xcalibur, who come out on stage to the theme song in a fantastic burst of glitz and glamour. Then the compère comes on and really warms the audience up, and then it is my turn. I stand behind the curtains while the music strikes up and the compère announces my name; each year I get the same nervous and yet excited feeling, but out I go. I introduce my team and welcome everyone and make my presentation. I refuse to stand behind a lectern and make a prepared speech; I use key cards in case I get stuck but I often forget to use them and just ad lib anyway. I also make short speeches in Danish, Dutch and German, which is often a worry because I am so afraid that my accent won't be understood.

Then I like to encourage the ladies to participate by taking the microphone down into the audience to talk to them. I think they really appreciate that, and I have come to realize that you really cannot motivate people as well from a remote stage.

In the evening we have a candlelit four-course dinner, which gives everyone a chance to really dress up and enjoy themselves. The dance troupes come back on and then there is a disco until 3 a.m. The dancing is choreographed and all looks very professional. Many of the ladies stay up until 5 a.m., they get such a buzz from the whole event. Every year the adrenaline and tension would build up in me and I never managed to last out to the end. But on the tenth anniversary I was determined to stay up, and I was still in the bar at 5 a.m. I could hardly get up the next morning to say goodbye because I was so exhausted.

Our conferences are always very slick and professional and we can afford to be much more outrageous with our unit organizers than we can with our customers. At the 1995 conference (our twelfth, held once again at the Birmingham Metropole) we used

Xperience and Xcalibur to launch the Erotica range, which is a combination of PVC, rubber and some very risqué garments in the main range and some very outrageous 'Still Life' products in the sex aids range. The ladies were left in no doubt about the message behind the launch! We thought that Ann Summers was becoming rather too conservative; we needed to remind people that it was all about fun. Julie had visited a few parties incognito and, acting on her advice, we decided to spice it all up a bit. We felt that we needed to bring home to the organizers the whole ethos of the company. It was a sort of 'Back to Basics' message with a difference!

The conference slogan was based on the high-impact hit song 'No Limits', which we felt was appropriate, and we chose a circus to demonstrate the idea of fun. The stage was designed like a circus ring and all the presenters were dressed for the part. Julie was typecast as a clown, and some of the others were acrobats and trapeze artists.

I was the ring master. I decided to go the whole hog on the outfit: I bought a long red jacket with a built-in waistcoat like a ringmaster's coat, black leggings, a white shirt, black lace-up boots and a very Liza Minelli-style black top hat, covered in sequins – a far cry from my usual business suit.

Of course, you can't be a ring master unless you have a whip, and I obviously had plenty to practise with (from the shops, I mean! They offer a full range, including one with a handle that looks like a black penis, which feels great to hold). And believe me, I needed lots of practice because I kept breaking the knotted ends off. (A word to the wise: it is all in the wrist movement! The skill is to drag it up very slowly and then, when you get to a certain height, just flick it hard.) I was practising everywhere and anywhere there was enough space – in the bedroom, the lounge, the hotel foyer. I think a few people felt that they had lucky escapes!

Getting the crack right became very important – each time I did it the ladies gave a cheer, and it became a personal morale-boosting crusade. The audience loved the theme and the way everyone was in on the act. I told them I felt like Miss Whiplash warming up for her next customer, and then reminded them how in the children's television show *Crackerjack*, Leslie Crowther would shout out the word and the children all shouted it back. The ladies caught on pretty quickly and now, even at meetings, if I say, 'No Limits!' they shout it right back at me. The following morning, when everyone was sitting in the breakfast room feeling a bit fragile, one woman came running in and shouted the slogan and, despite their hangovers, they all screamed it back.

Before we had decided on the circus theme I had invited Richard Berry, Chairman of the DSA, along. He always sees me in a professional, business-like environment and I think he was very surprised, to say the least, when he saw me up on the stage, cracking a whip!

After I had done my introduction I called for the executive team, who all came out wearing normal clothes, but with funny hats and noses. We had rehearsed it all carefully and, as planned, Julie came on last in her full clown's outfit. The audience went wild; they all love Julie and were delighted to see her dressed up too. Julie made as if to leave the stage, but I called her back and said, 'Hang on: do you remember when I did my dance routine, I said I would get you to tap dance this year?' and she shook her head and pretended to look aghast. Then, like in a pantomime, I asked the ladies to shout if they wanted her to dance, and she launched into this tap dance routine – quite an undertaking with great long clown's feet!

The ladies said afterwards that this was the best conference ever because they felt so involved. Keith Chegwin was our compère and he was the best we have ever had. The ladies warmed to him instantly because he spontaneously ran all these on-the-spot competitions, offering Big Breakfast mugs and T-shirts for the woman who could reach highest in the room (we had ladies standing on the tables, with other ladies on their shoulders! – my heart was in my mouth), and for the table (of ten ladies) who could all get underneath the table and the tablecloth without any part of them

Left: 'Susannah' from the Twice as Sexy Collection for fuller figures. Available in sizes 16 to 28, the collection was introduced in 1991 following feedback from customers.

Right: 'Faye', a bestseller at Ann Summers for five years.

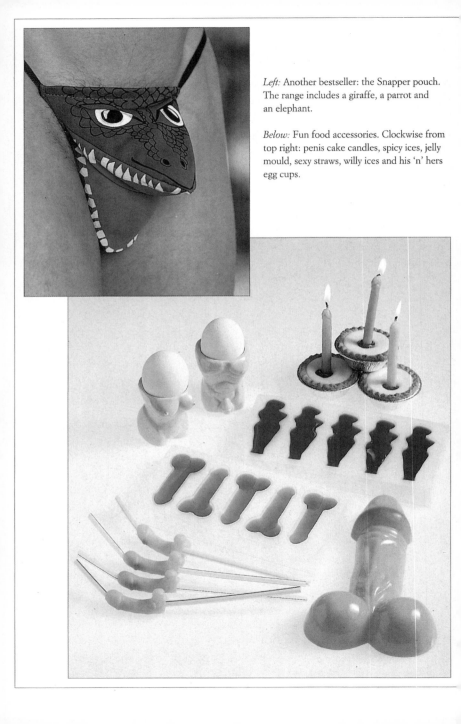

Left: Another bestseller: the Snapper pouch. The range includes a giraffe, a parrot and an elephant.

Below: Fun food accessories. Clockwise from top right: penis cake candles, spicy ices, jelly mould, sexy straws, willy ices and his 'n' hers egg cups.

My philosophy has always been to encourage women to feel good about themselves and their sexuality.
(© Brian Aris)

Two covers from *Bite*, my magazine for women. I really wanted it to be a success, but insurmountable problems meant it only ran for a year.

Expressions

ESSENTIAL FOR WOMEN, IRRESISTIBLE TO MEN

Tarnished Gold

Family pornographic empire
that lies behind the success of
Ann Summers boss Jacqueline

By NORMAN LUCK and VICTORIA HARPER

JACQUELINE GOLD, famed for a top business award, is far from the normal gift-giving queen of industry commended for her services.

True, the 33-year-old beauty looks like James Bond's Miss Moneypenny, with her hair and stylish clothes, but behind the calm smile and Yves St Laurent power suit is a legacy of male titillation.

Jacqueline comes from a family up to its G-strings in pornography. She is the figurehead and a major shareholder for Gold Star Publications, an organisation that sells sex right out of the Paul Raymond mould.

Don't be fooled by her winning smile and soft dimples — they form the family's drive to widen sexual fantasies for men and women throughout Britain. Although Jacqueline doesn't talk much about it.

Her business skills won her a pioneering prize this week at the Women Mean Business Awards, sponsored by Options magazine and Volkshonne Television. But the prestigious event brought red faces at the West London headquarters of the magazine after Jacqueline's ties with a leading porn baron were discovered.

Maureen Rice, editor of Options, who decided that out of 700 applications the Ann Summers boss of the year should be put forward as a candidate for the award, admits she didn't know about Jacqueline Gold's porn background.

"I didn't realise that Gold Star was the holding company until yesterday after a conversation with Jacqueline who told me that she had shares in Gold Star."

Later Miss Rice, after a call from the Ann Summers organisation, contacted the Daily Express to make clear: "We made the award to Jacqueline Gold for her success in running the Ann Summers Party Plan. We were impressed that she runs a company operated run by women for women and she employs 7,500 women.

"I must worry you I am feeling like telephone call led me are recording every word of this

SHOPFRONT: Ann Summers store in London's Soho

TITILLATION: Catalogues of the company's range

BIG BUSINESS: Ann Summers Surrey headquarters

to customers behind others. We were judging Jacqueline solely on the merit of Ann Summers which is a very successful and well-run company.

"We chose her because her application was so strong. We are never going to close down our sex industry so no business for women, that way Ann Summers does, has got to be a positive thing."

When asked whether she thought that it was appropriate

to comment, saying that she would need to consider it more carefully.

She went on to say: "Women want to be attractive and there is nothing wrong with it. Women feel too intimidated to go into sex shops themselves by buying it in this way a lot of women feel they can freely express themselves. A sex business run for women and by women is a great thing." Other applica-

---

Negative and positive: the Daily Express *published conflicting stories about me on consecutive days.*

Daily Express

WEDNESDAY SEPTEMBER 22 1993   WEATHER: SUNNY SPELLS   32p

£250,000 MUST BE WON
IT'S YOUR CHANCE TO BE RICH   SEE PAGES FOR TODAY'S TOKEN

Turmoil in the Kremlin as troops move
on Moscow and parliament is suspended

YELTSIN'S HUGE GAMBLE

BORIS: Plea to world

From WILL STEWART in Moscow

CRACK troops moved into Moscow last night to back Boris Yeltsin as he seized emergency powers to run Russia as a dictatorship.

The president took a massive gamble, risking civil war, when he suspended the old-guard parliament.

His dramatic move made him the nation's most powerful man since Stalin and triggered a fight to the finish with his political enemies.

Yeltsin, who promised new elections in December, pleaded for international support in a TV broadcast from the Kremlin.

He was met with immediate defiance from rivals who have been blocking his sweeping economic reforms.

Accused

Rebel vice-president Alexander Rutskoi insisted that he, not Yeltsin, is now the legitimate ruler of Russia.

He accused the Kremlin chief of a coup d'état. "We must act now to stop a slide towards civil war," he said.

Rutskoi said SAS-style troops loyal to Yeltsin were marching on Moscow. Hardliners began building barricades around the parliament building.

There were reports of large military deployments in and around the city.

Tension mounted further as parliament later named Rutskoi as acting president.

Its chairman Ruslan Khasbulatov urged the army and police to ignore Yeltsin's orders. "I turn to all servicemen

Page 2 Column 2

What the sex queen promised Secretary of State

by MICHAEL O'FLAHERTY

SEX queen Jacqueline Gold met Health Secretary Virginia Bottomley yesterday — and promised to send her something to the statesy women's mags.

Mrs Bottomley obviously did not ask for an Ann Summers catalogue, which contains a variety of erotics and sex aids known — and welcomes — to men (this one at least).

But she will be getting one anyway, promised the mini-skirted boss of the sex shop chain.

"It will be in the post tonight," she told the Minister.

Poor Mrs Bottomley. When she met Jacqueline at a business women's awards ceremony yesterday, a few key words gushed.

"Hello, nice to meet you," a primly-dressed Mrs Bottomley told the entirely airy figure in a cheeky red suit.

Pause. "Congratulations." Then the Health Secretary walked her bemused smile to the presented Jacqueline with a Working Woman award.

Page 3 Column 3

BROUGHT TO BOOK: Jacqueline Gold at the ceremony yesterday with Mrs Bottomley

Pictured as one of the Gucci/*Business Age* '40 under 40' most successful managers and entrepreneurs in 1994. (© *Business Age*)

My mother Beryl when she married John on 3rd July 1989.

Another of my favourite photos: me, aged five, with my Dad.

Dad (right) and his brother Ralph (left) pictured with Barry Fry at Birmingham City Football Club after the Club won the Auto Windscreen Shield at Wembley in April 1995. The Gold brothers have a 50 per cent stake in the Blues, and are loyal fans.

Relaxed and looking forward to the future.

showing, which occasioned a great deal of elbowing and giggling! It was all down to audience participation and team work. I think Keith had a really great time too.

The compère is generally chosen from nominations from the party organizers. Year after year, without fail, the most popular compère on the list is Michael Barrymore; we would love to have him but he is just too expensive, which is a shame because I am sure he would be excellent. Other suggestions – including one for Meatloaf – have been rather less serious. One thing we have learned is that you cannot always tell who is going to be good just by watching them on television.

Each year we agonize about how to improve on the previous year's great success. My theory is that when you have reached a level of perfection within your budget and your theme, then the only way to improve is by changing and making it as different as possible. At Ann Summers the last thing we want to become is predictable.

Chapter Nine
GOOD VIBRATIONS

OUR CATALOGUES and the range they offer have always been important to me – as important as the Annual Conference – because I regard them very much as our shop window. When our customers are sitting in someone's home, flicking through the pages, I want them to see something that they like and at least something else that titillates and amuses them.

The walls outside my office are lined with the covers of all our catalogues over the years: it is like a social history of changing sexual attitudes in Britain, starting with the baby-doll look of the seventies, through the more raunchy style of the eighties to the sophisticated, feminine look of the late eighties and nineties.

We take a great deal of time and trouble over the models and the lingerie range and play products, from the way they look and what they cost to their names and the wording of the descriptions. As anyone glancing at our catalogue will gather, we also have a great deal of fun! Here, for example, are the descriptions of some of our fun and personal products:

- **Glow Condom** – the ideal way to light up your love life.
- **Parrot Pouch** – here's something to keep his pecker up.
- **For the Man Who Likes a Blow Job** – what else but a hand-kerchief?
- **Sperm Bank** – deposit or withdraw with this cheeky pottery money box.

- **Ankle Penis** – win friends and influence people, strap this joke penis to your ankle and watch your popularity soar.
- **Foreskin Vibrator** – incredible seven-inch vibrator with realistic skin movement.

In the old days the most popular vibrators were the simple seven-inch ribbed version (the Humming Bird), and the Ladies Secret, a five-inch vibrator with matching case that looked more like a perfume or a large lipstick than a sex aid. Women are far more selective and discerning now. Many customers own three or more vibrators and at parties they openly discuss which is the best and why. (The best way to test a vibrator in public, incidentally, is to hold it lightly against the tip of your nose to feel the level of vibration.)

The fun items, like the chocolate nipples and the penis-shaped ice-cube containers, are extremely popular as birthday or Christmas gifts, or as presents for hen and stag nights. One of our best sellers is the Snapper Pouch, a posing pouch with an alligator's open mouth on it. We even sell a very popular board game called 'Fantasy for Lovers' which was actually created and put together by Ralph. The catalogue describes it as 'the most daring game you will ever play, win or lose'.

In addition to the fun we have making up the names and descriptions, behind the scenes we also examine some products which are too raunchy or shocking, even for us! One manufacturer recently sent us a very strange kit which featured a velcro headband with a miner's-type lamp on the front and gynaecological implements 'for the man who wants to get to know his partner better'! I mean, I ask you! It could only have been invented by a man! From America we were sent the Organ-Izer, which was a sort of elaborate vacuum pump canister to place over a penis to get it erect and hold it there indefinitely, and the Double Dong, a double-ended twelve-inch-long rubber willy, for two girls together! I can hardly mention some of the other products, like the

Vibro Sandy; suffice to say that the fake hair always seems to come off! Goodness knows what the product testers would think ... Yes, we do have product testers – Ann Summers women all over the country who selflessly test our products after they have passed all the British electrical standards tests at head office. This dedicated band of volunteers boldly go where no man has gone before, and report back to head office on the effectiveness of a product. Their names and addresses are confidential and are known by only a few key senior staff. None of them admits to what she does; one apparently tells friends and neighbours she does market research for an electrical company!

With suggestions and offers coming in from manufacturers from as far away as Taiwan, it is also very easy for the staff involved to get carried away and choose just what they like, so I remain closely involved to remind everyone that we do have customers! We have considered opening a Black Museum of all those items that didn't make it past the purchasing team – I think we'd have people queuing for miles!

We currently produce two bumper catalogues a year, one for the autumn/winter season and one for spring/summer, in addition to other special supplements – we produce two million copies of the Christmas one. Vanessa oversees the design and the selection of the models and the items, although I have the final say. The whole thing is now run in a very structured way: first we have a catalogue development meeting with Vanessa, the Merchandising Manager and the Buyer, to review the latest report and the trends of the season. Our business is seasonal but we get round that by offering special promotions (in the summer we have our swimwear range, for example). October and November are our exceptional months. Even in underwear the fashions change very quickly: this year, because of the success of the Gossard Wonderbra ads, everything is very structured and Brigitte Bardot-like and we have seen a surge in bras. A few years ago, during the Madonna phase, basques and boned bustiers were all the rage.

The catalogue changes and adapts as best it can to the trends, which is why we bring out two a year. We obviously have to discontinue some items – usually the poorest sellers – to make room for the new ones. We also take into consideration things like cost, poor availability and quality problems on a certain line. We avoid having too much overstock by offering discontinued items as gifts or special offers to our girls or sending it abroad: this year's overstock in the UK may be next year's hot item in another country. The last thing we want is for Ann Summers lingerie to turn up on some market stall at a reduced price. If we ever find out that is happening, incidentally, we come down very hard and always prosecute, so market traders beware!

On the lingerie, we try to be as competitive as possible with our direct rivals. We have to make sure that there is something for everybody: once, before I knew better, I just discontinued the items that were at the bottom of the sales list, completely overlooking the fun element of the whole business. There will always be some items that have to be included whether or not they are in the top forty, simply because people expect them to be there and because they form an important part of the whole Party Plan concept. Women may not buy the very daring products but they expect to see them on offer and enjoy having a good look and a feel and a laugh. It is all part of the entertainment value of Ann Summers. Our customers want to be slightly shocked; I would be alarmed if I thought the range was acceptable to everybody.

So we always have what we call our 'Outrageous Products' on offer; these are generally brought out towards the end of the party when everyone is warmed up and having a good time. The very latest Outrageous Product is the Emperor vibrator, which is an eight-inch vibrator with the shape and feel of a real penis, complete with blue veins and everything. It certainly caused a stir at head office when it came in. It has a suction pad on its base so it can be stuck on the wall or the coffee table or anywhere you like. A woman who bought one at a party recently announced that she planned to sit on it while she was watching *Neighbours* and doing her ironing. I don't think her husband's shirts will get too much attention from now on!

Another Outrageous Product is the Talking Vibrator, which is quite life-like and features a man's voice egging the woman on to sexual climax. It is surprisingly popular, although I understand that the voice sometimes becomes rather muffled! This item caused me a very embarrassing moment: one of my buying team gave me a talking vibrator – along with a whole range of other products from this particular manufacturer – to take home and look at. I asked her to put all the goods in the boot of my car and, quite forgetting they were there, I parked in Harley Street and went off shopping, returning later with a few carrier bags. It was the start of the evening rush hour and hundreds of people were coming out of offices near by.

As I opened the boot of my car I (along with everyone else walking past) was greeted by this man's voice saying: 'Yes! yes! yes! Come on baby, I'm a cock, make me come.' The voice went on and on, getting more and more excited. Several people – totally astounded – stopped to look and listen some more. As for me, I was so flustered I couldn't think straight. The sensible thing to have done was to slam the boot shut and drive off, but in my panic I rummaged my way through the box of vibrators and other sex aids until I found the one that was talking and managed to switch it off. It was deeply embarrassing and I have never been able to park in Harley Street since.

It is almost worse when people know what you do for a living. I remember going to Jersey with Stuart and a group of his friends; we were at the airport going through customs when there was this buzzing in one of the bags. I looked at Stuart and he looked at me, and all his friends and the customs men looked at us both and I knew exactly what they were all thinking. But when Stuart opened the bag to see, it was just his electric razor. I could have killed him, I was so embarrassed; his friends kept giving me strange looks for the rest of the weekend.

When we brought out the Talking Vibrator it caused quite a stir and reached the attention of the national press. One of my all-time favourite newspaper articles about Ann Summers appeared in the Sunday tabloid the *People*. The headline ran: 'NEW WILLY IS TALKING MEN OUT OF A JOB':

Thousands of raunchy women have been snapping up a talking vibrator which moans, groans and tells them they are beautiful. The mind-boggling sex aid has taken Britain's housewives by storm and suppliers Ann Summers are struggling to keep up with demand.

One customer was so thrilled with the pink, eight-inch sex toy that she said: 'It's much better than a man. It keeps going all night and doesn't roll over and go to sleep after. This could be the end of men in the bedroom.'

Since its launch just a few months ago, an incredible 30,000 have been sold at £24.99 each. Women at Ann Summers parties say they are turned on by a husky male voice that moans in ecstasy whenever it is switched on. The mystery hunk whispers passionately: 'Oh yeah, come on, ooh aah.' And then it works up to a climax with: 'Oh God, oh yeah, come on, you're beautiful. Mmmmm.'

One satisfied 38-year-old from Watford, Herts, said in a letter to Ann Summers headquarters: 'It says all the right things, never breaks wind at vital moments and doesn't tell me to shave my legs. I've recommended it to all my friends and carry it round in my handbag, just in case.'

We asked men and women what they thought the rubber willy *should* say and here's what they told us:

MEN: 'Get us a cup of tea, luv.'
'Fancy a pizza now?'
'Can I go for a pint yet?'
'Got to go — *Match of the Day's* on. Zzzzzzzzzzzzzzz.'

WOMEN: 'God, you've got a wonderful body.'
'You smell so sexy.'
'Who cares, let the phone ring.'
'I've recorded *Coronation Street*.'
'Of course you won't get pregnant.'

(4 April 1995. Reproduced by kind permission of Bridget Rowe, Editor, the *People*.)

The last but by absolutely no means the least of our Outrageous Products is an item called the Tongue. It was sent in by a supplier in Hong Kong and I knew it would be a winner the moment it arrived because you could hear the shrieks of laughter and surprise as soon as my staff pulled it out of the box. Whatever it was, if that was the reaction in the office, the women at the parties would go wild. I was right; it really is our party piece – a huge life-like tongue with a tip that wiggles around. It is quite revolting really, all pocked like a real tongue and pale pink, but it is quite a conversation stopper. We do have to be careful what we sell and try not to offend. Women find the Tongue hilarious, but men think it's repulsive. Even Stuart, who is entirely comfortable with what I sell, was disgusted when I brought it home one night to show him. He asked me in horror, 'Do people really use that?'

We launched the swimwear catalogue in February 1991 after I had received hundreds of letters from the girls asking for a swimwear range. I encourage letters from everyone within Ann Summers and write a piece at the beginning of each catalogue specifically asking for feedback. I acknowledge all the letters I receive: I do think that if someone has taken the trouble to write they should get a response.

We didn't have any swimwear suppliers to start with; initially our buying team went to our existing manufacturers and asked them to make the swimwear up for us. This was a disaster because they were lingerie specialists; they were not geared up for swimwear and it showed. We also guessed wrongly at the market and ordered a lot of swimwear with thongs because we thought the customers would want risqué swimwear. Of course you have to look like a model to wear a thong in public and the custom just wasn't there. The first range did not do very well at all.

The second swimwear range was far more successful. We rectified all the previous year's mistakes and it has gone from strength to strength and now appears as a separate supplement. We still carry the thongs, but they are not generally bought for the beach; women tend to wear them in the bedroom or under clothes. Much of our swimwear doubles up as tops and evening wear.

In March 1992 I launched our Twice as Sexy range of underwear in sizes 16 to 28 for our larger customers. We had been toying with the idea for some time and had already increased our size range, but I was really inspired by one particular woman who wrote in to me. I had received lots of letters requesting larger sizes of sexy underwear, but this lady intrigued me: she was a widow and had no man in her life at all. In a very frank letter, she said that just because she was alone now, it didn't mean she no longer needed nice underwear to make herself feel sexy; she wasn't going to put on her thermals just because there was no one to see her undressed. This letter confirmed my suspicions – that women don't buy sexy underwear just to please their men; they buy it primarily for themselves (with their partner in mind, of course) to make themselves feel confident and sexy.

After we had launched the range, which went down a storm and sells very well indeed, I had a lovely letter from one lady who said she had just lost a few stone but, having seen the new underwear, was tempted to put all the weight back on again! 'At last someone has realized that larger women love luxurious and lovely lingerie and that they too can be glamorous and sexy,' she wrote. 'My fiancé agrees, so maybe I will abandon diets and just be my normal curvy self.' It was typical of a lot of the letters we get from larger women. Personally I don't think men really do want skinny women; I think they like a few curves.

We launched the Erotica range at the 1995 AGC. This was really quite raunchy wear, and I was concerned that it might be a step backwards to the raincoat brigade days. But, after talking to our customers and organizers I realized that things have changed dramatically since then: some items in the range would have been considered far too outrageous a few years ago; moreover, women are now buying these items for themselves, and are no longer being typecast by men. It takes time, but we are finally redressing the balance.

Women of the nineties are very much more aware of their sexuality and many are much more confident in the bedroom than they were fifteen years ago. I believe a lot of women rediscover themselves in their late twenties: before then they have fantasies about being more adventurous, but only later do they find the confidence to make those fantasies come true.

One of the items that we only sell in the shops is the blow-up doll —mainly because they wouldn't sell very well: at parties they are quite expensive (£30–£400). A blow-up doll is really for a man to use and there is not much point in having them at our parties. We did and do sell some male blow-up dolls, but we have had innumerable problems with their manufacture. One batch arrived without any willies at all and we had to send them back. When the next lot arrived we thought that the same thing had happened, only to discover that the willies had been tucked up inside the models for easy packaging!

One true story which I like to tell the organizers at meetings is about an organizer called Sheena. The story came from a newspaper cutting which was then used in our in-house magazine, *Network*. Sheena was driving to an Ann Summers party on her moped, but was stopped by the police because she was carrying a passenger on the back (as a learner she is not allowed to do this). When the policemen approached the moped they realized, to their horror, that the passenger was not a person at all but a blow-up doll. Sheena told them: 'I always take Belinda to parties like this – it saves blowing her up all the time, and she travels better fully inflated!' I can't help but laugh when I imagine the policemen's faces. After that article appeared, I learned that quite a few of the girls buy blow-up dolls to take along to the parties as a fun way of modelling the underwear.

We have had several requests for a vibrating blow-up man, which many women said they would prefer to their husbands, but we have never found a good enough design to make it viable! Now that security companies in Europe and America are selling blow-up men to sit alongside lone women driving at night, however, we might look into it again and devise a multi-purpose blow-up man – for that feeling of comfort and security in the car or at home!

There was once a newspaper headline about me which read something like: 'SHE SELLS 50p VIBRATORS FOR £10.95'; it was a ridiculous set of figures to pluck from the air and it really annoyed me. If only it were true. There is obviously a mark-up on the goods we buy in and then sell – we wouldn't make any money at all if there wasn't – but what people forget is that we are like wholesalers: we sell goods to the organizers for 30 per cent less, and they make their money by selling it on at the catalogue price. But even with their percentage and ours, we still have to be aware of what our customers are prepared to pay.

I am constantly meeting people who are prejudiced against the sex industry and a woman running a business. There are some who made me feel very proud of my achievements, but I am dogged by snide remarks about the business I run. In many ways, I think it is an added pressure for me because I know how hard won our success was and is. People come up and chat to me and I can instantly sense their caginess: either they look me up and down rather strangely and make innuendoes or they just come out with all the old jokes. I am often asked if I wear the underwear we sell (of course, I do!) and who chooses and tests the products (the suggestion is that I test and choose all the vibrators myself!) – all with a twinkle in the eye of course. I just have to learn to live with it and not take offence.

Another question I am asked is if I have mirrors on the ceiling above my bed, which I always find quite funny. The answer is emphatically no. I think most people would be surprised and disappointed if they came to my house. It is very feminine, and I have cuddly toys and embroideries, not satin sheets and phallic soaps. Naturally everyone wants to know if I use a vibrator. I refuse to answer this question because it is quite nice to keep people guessing. If I said, 'Yes,' everyone would say, 'I told you so,' and if I said, 'No,' they wouldn't believe me. I quite like the mystique and I don't mind the innuendoes, but I always leave it at that. I will say, however, that I don't think I am different to any other woman, and I think sex is great. I also love sexy underwear, particularly the thongs – not so much for their comfort or because I have a particularly good bottom, but because I hate to see a panty line through clothes. I probably have the largest range of underwear of any woman I know because of the business I am in. No man has ever bought me underwear; I suppose everyone thinks I probably have enough. I think it is wonderful when a man buys something so intimate for a woman. He is really saying, 'I find you really attractive and I think you would look very sexy in this.'

I haven't become immune to sex because of what I do. When a relationship is new, the sex is new and buzzing (if you will excuse the expression!); when the relationship deteriorates, the sex often deteriorates with it. The chemistry obviously has to be right in the first place, but I think you have to be in love with someone for it to be really special.

Prejudices emerge in the most unexpected places. I was dining at a posh restaurant with some business colleagues once and ordered a fruit salad for dessert. The waiter must have known who I was because he looked at me meaningfully and said: 'And I'll make sure the chef includes a banana in that for you.' I mean, I ask you!

On another occasion, I needed some curtains for these big picture windows in my lounge at home and I called in an interior designer. My house is very soft and feminine – pinks and blues, peaches and creams, with soft carpets and floral prints. Anyone who walked in should have known what type of thing I wanted. I had asked the man to bring some designs for me to look at. I didn't know him, but it soon became obvious that he knew me and knew what I did, because he started showing me all these bold colours with frills and lace – they were completely over the top – and telling me that this or that design was 'very sexy'. Sexy! Curtains? I couldn't believe it; here I was being pressed into choosing something *he* thought the Managing Director of Ann Summers would like.

In 1992 I decided that I wanted to open a chain of lingerie shops – just lingerie, nothing else – and I visited shopping precincts to look at sites. I thought I would start with the Glades Shopping Centre in Bromley and arranged to meet a rep from the company handling the sites. I found a suitable one next to Marks & Spencer, so I told him I was ready to go. I suddenly sensed that there was a problem, and I was right because all at once he started saying to me that the owners were not happy with Ann Summers being in the shopping centre; the product was fine, apparently, but I could only have the shop if I changed its name from Ann Summers Lingerie to something else. I couldn't believe it! The whole point of the shop was to have the Ann Summers logo on it: I wanted to attract both established and new customers. The rep left me completely stunned, but his female assistant commented: 'I honestly don't know what all the fuss is about. I have been to lots of your parties and they are great fun.' That really epitomized the difference between male and female attitudes to Ann Summers. Here we were, in the middle of a recession, and this guy was moralizing over a name.

We see that sort of attitude almost exclusively in men who are uncomfortable with the product and what we do for women and their confidence. I wouldn't compromise as a matter of principle: if you start compromising on something like that, then where do you stop?

We also encounter some resistance from some of the older

guard, and from the husbands and boyfriends of our female customers, which I find extraordinary in this day and age. Our battle for acceptance by women has largely been won, but we still find that men feel threatened by Ann Summers and the women who are involved in it. Women are taking control of their sex lives, but men are worrying that their girlfriends or wives will find a vibrator more satisfying than them. They cannot imagine it being a shared, mutually satisfying sexual experience.

This clash of interests was brought home to me recently at the opening of one of the newly refurbished shops. A couple were walking past the window and I heard the woman say: 'Oh look, it's Ann Summers – they sell vibrators, let's go in.' But the man gripped her by the arm and said: 'It's either me or the vibrator, we are moving on,' and frogmarched her off! Another couple outside the shop had an argument which became so heated that the Area Manager had to ask them to leave. The man didn't want to go in and he refused to look after the children outside while his wife went in. And this is supposed to be the liberated nineties!

At times like that I am grateful for the mail order side of the business: women like the ones I saw arguing with their men can have access to the product without having to go into a shop. Mail order is also available to party customers who would rather order by mail than direct from the organizer. The mail order business was around long before Party Plan and is still profitable. Turnover is about £1 million a year.

Of course I receive innumerable suggestions from men. Most of the letters are pretty harmless requests for advice, but recently I came across one which I just couldn't decipher because the handwriting was so bad and the spelling atrocious. I passed it on to Carol, my PA, with one of those little yellow sticky notes saying: 'I can't make out what this man wants.' That afternoon the letter came back with a sticky note from Carol in reply: 'We know what he wants and he is not going to get it!'

One place I encounter very few prejudices is at a Direct Selling Association conference. Not only do I feel welcome, I find the atmosphere very motivating. Once a year there is a conference in the States and I always return with all these fantastic ideas. Unfortunately the systems are very behind the times over here. For example, a few years ago I wanted to introduce credit card sales for customers buying at parties but neither Access nor Visa would do business with us. We approached them again three years later and came across countless stumbling blocks – the main one being that we needed 7,500 swipe machines and training for all our ladies, and with a large number of new organizers joining each month it was a logistical nightmare.

At a DSA American conference I also discovered that in the US there was a system that replaces credit card machines with a type of cheque book which has duplicate paper in it. The credit card is placed under the copy paper and rubbed with a special pen. The trace that is left is like the undercopy you currently get from a normal credit card transaction. I thought it was brilliant and perfect for our needs, but when I came back to Britain with the idea the banks and the credit card companies just wouldn't have it. It was too progressive for them. So instead, we follow a telephone ordering system for credit cards, which is all very long-winded in terms of paper and administration.

The Orderline is another project we are constantly updating. We started with about two members of staff to answer the phone and tap all the orders into a computer. Now we have about seventeen. I am currently looking into IVR, a voice-activated telephone system to run alongside our current system, where you phone a special answerphone and give your answers at the appropriate moment via your telephone buttons. This is something I would like to get in place soon, but we will have to do some research first to see if customers feel happy talking to a machine.

Because of the cost involved we are one of the few UK companies who go to the American conference, but I feel the US input is very important as the workshops are informative and energetic. I always take Julie with me and we split up and participate in as many as possible. We always come home with lots of ideas and enthusiasm. The DSA is very important to me. I was on the 1995 conference committee and some time soon it will be Ann Summers's turn to organize the whole thing, which will be quite an undertaking.

Chapter Ten
ONCE BITTEN

MY RELATIONSHIP with the press over the years has, on the whole, been very positive and productive. A few minor injustices aside, I feel I have been very lucky because I have built up a good rapport with journalists. I have always been pretty up-front and honest and they seem to respect me for that.

It all started in 1992, when the *Independent on Sunday* contacted me and said they would like an interview. My father and Ralph had always shunned publicity and the Gold Group had a policy of no comment, so nobody knew very much about what we did. I was a bit apprehensive about doing the interview, but I enjoy new experiences and I thought it would be good for the business. I had assumed that I would do the interview and that would be that, but suddenly everything just snowballed and I was news.

The media is always on the look-out for a new personality, a face to put to a product, and I was a good prospect: I photograph quite well and I was not at all the bold and brassy woman they expected. The story was a winner. Once the newsdesks had seen my picture and realized what I sold, I had a profile, and within a few weeks I was inundated with requests for interviews. It overwhelmed me, my family and my staff and so I decided to sign up with a public relations company.

The first one we used seemed enthusiastic but before long the bills started to come in and I thought that if we were going to spend this much money – up to £4,000 a month – we should insist on a better service. I always felt that PRs were so phoney and snobbish. I hated all that insincere gush. They didn't really want to dirty their hands with Ann Summers but they couldn't resist the opportunity of a quick earner. I went through company after company, and they were all as bad as each other.

I knew that I had to find someone good, so I started shopping around. One person I went to see was Max Clifford, who was relatively unknown before Antonia de Sancha and David Mellor. For a number of reasons he was not right for me, so I decided to take on our own in-house PR person. I remember Max had proposed to sit in on every interview and fend off any awkward questions. I had considered that quite unnecessary, but late one night I found myself being interviewed alone by a woman reporter from a tabloid newspaper.

She was very intrusive and wanted to send a photographer round to do shots of me in my underwear, which I had flatly refused. All of a sudden, she reached under the table and started running her hand along my leg. I froze. I remember thinking: 'My God, Max, where are you? All is forgiven!' I was stunned, but I knew that if I got up and walked out she could write a negative piece about me. So I simply asked her what she thought she was doing. 'Oh, it's all right, daahling,' she purred. 'I was just feeling to see if you were wearing stockings or tights.'

I wanted to throw her out, but I knew I couldn't, so I bit my lip and crossed my legs well away from her and carried on. After she had gone I was quite relieved!

Not long after that I took on Jacquie Wilson, a bright and bubbly Scottish girl who had previously worked at Hallmark Cards. I liked her instantly and found her refreshingly genuine after all the fakes I had been dealing with. What she lacked in experience, she made up for in enthusiasm and energy, but I believe that is sometimes all to the good.

I also decided to get some proper media training and went to London to see a man who had trained key politicians. It cost £1,000 for one day's training, but as I wanted to learn very quickly

I thought it would be money well spent. In the event I felt the whole day was a waste of time. After that I went to see a woman called Brenda. She was great but she was a real bully. She set me up in a mock television studio for an interview and just launched into me with questions like: 'You are just peddling sex, aren't you?' and 'When did you lose your virginity?' She went on and on attacking me about pornography and how I was exploiting women. She simply ate me alive. When they played the video of the interview back I could see it was a disaster. I was so defensive and my eyes were darting all over the place. I looked like a frightened rabbit caught in the car headlights.

Brenda taught me how to 'bridge' – to create a break while I thought out my answer – and how not to answer questions if I didn't want to. I learned not to be defensive and was shown the importance of body language. I really did learn a lot. She set up another television interview to put me to the test. This time it was going really well until she suddenly dreamed up this scenario where an MP was found dead in kinky underwear; she suggested that if it wasn't for companies like mine people wouldn't do this sort of thing, and I went to pieces again!

Around this time Julie and I went to see a colour analyst, who talked about corporate dress. She was a bit extreme – all pin-stripe suits and power dressing. At this stage in my career I was anxious to be taken seriously, so I immediately went in for very severe suits and hairstyles. I wore glasses, not contact lenses, and one of the newspapers said I looked like Miss Moneypenny, the prim and proper secretary from the James Bond films, which was about right.

The first television programme I appeared on was *Good Morning Britain* with Lorraine Kelly. One reviewer said I looked like a politician, so I never wore my hair up again. In an effort to be taken seriously, I had compromised my femininity. I hardly ever wear my hair up now and discourage other women from making the same mistake as I did.

The media could not at first accept that I was normal. I remember during one particular photo shoot I had to rest my hands on the belts of these half-naked male models. Afterwards a reporter asked me if it had turned me on, which I found very objectionable. I was not the expected Miss Whiplash, so I had to be the exact opposite. Some journalists also seemed to think I was embarrassed about my own product. I may be selective in the words I use to describe the sex aids – 'play products', 'novelties' and 'personal products' – but I am certainly in no way ashamed of them.

Inspired by my dealings with the media and bolstered by the growing success of the company, I decided to go ahead with my long-cherished plan to publish a magazine for women. My family have always been in publishing and I felt that there was a niche for what I referred to not as a women's adult magazine, but an adult women's magazine.

The result was *Bite*, a middle-shelf women's magazine that offered more than, say, *Cosmopolitan*, but was less hard-core than the sexually explicit *For Women*. Magazines like *For Women* were always positioned on the top shelf – mainly, I felt, because they featured full-nude males. But most women could not physically reach them, and were uncomfortable with buying them in a newsagent. I wanted to bring out something that really addressed the sexual issues and interests of women. I was also toying with the idea of marketing such a magazine through the Party Plan, but I later realized that most of our customers read *Best* and *Bella*.

At about this time the Print Production Manager at Gold Star told me that two women had come to see him about publishing a magazine they had provisionally called *Gigi*. I had a couple of meetings with them and they put together a proposal, but in the end I decided not to go ahead because their format had more in common with *For Women* than the more sophisticated publication I had in mind. But meeting them inspired me. I was even more convinced that my idea would work, and so was everyone around me. I asked for a costing package and decided to go ahead at a set-up cost of £250,000. We advertised for an editor and chose a woman called Catherine Handcock. From our offices in Caledonian Road, London, she then recruited her team of about six staff. Right from the start I was very hands on – this was something I really wanted to shape. We had a lot of meetings and I approved the covers and a lot of the material that went inside.

Initially we had to play it very carefully. Our main aim was obviously to get the major retailers like W. H. Smith and Menzies to sell it, but because they had their own preconceived ideas about Ann Summers they insisted on copy approval. If the magazine was to succeed, I had no choice but to accept their terms until we had proved ourselves, so we tried to anticipate what they would or wouldn't object to.

Our first edition was billed as 'the first magazine to redefine sex' and came out in May 1993. Our rivals were a little twitchy at first; their covers argued: 'It is not all about sex' and 'Why women should adopt the missionary position' (which was actually about voluntary work overseas!). We had promised to deliver what was advertised on our cover, and the first edition had a feature entitled: 'Fellatio: the Definitive User's Guide', and a reader's test on condoms.

The media gave the magazine a good reception and we had a champagne launch party for over 300 people. I felt very satisfied. I could see *Bite* raising Ann Summers's profile generally; I wanted it to reflect the ethos of the Party Plan – an honest, up-front, intelligent and informed approach to sex in the nineties. We sold about 100,000 copies of the first issue. After the first few months it settled at around 70,000, and things seemed to be going well. But then sales started to dwindle to about 40,000 a month (we knew we had to sell 80,000 to break even).

At an early stage, the editorial team and I started to have serious differences of opinion. When you have a team not on site, not directly under your nose, you never have the same control. The magazine contained a lot of strong swear words which I felt were unnecessary. I was also unhappy with the covers, which were just not matching up to my perception of the magazine. It seemed too much like a college rag-mag — too bitty and arty-farty and feministic. After a while I realized that the team had their own agenda for it. The PR and advertising companies were being influenced by this view and no one seemed to have any real understanding of who the customer was or what she wanted.

I have built up Ann Summers on the basis of what the customer wants, and I do have a pretty good idea of the sex industry from a woman's point of view. The magazine had been set up to harness that knowledge and put it to commercial use, but the team didn't seem to see it that way. I think they were embarrassed about being associated with Ann Summers.

We were getting good feedback about the content, but the layout was wrong and the magazine was generally too inconsistent. I desperately wanted to rectify all of that but it was such a struggle that there was no fun in it. Meetings at the magazine's offices were tense and the team were fiercely protective of their product.

The magazine lasted just a year in spite of all my efforts to save it. I hired a troubleshooter called Richard Proctor who had been instrumental in setting up *Hello!* magazine. He was very open and honest with me and endorsed my view of things; I wished I had had him on board from the beginning. It is very difficult to troubleshoot when the trouble has already crippled you. We looked at new forecasts and costings and advertising campaigns and he worked very hard trying to hold it all together. We discovered that many newsagents were putting *Bite* on the top shelf despite all our entreaties, and that drastically affected sales. We met with Smiths and the distributors, but we had no influence by the time some provincial shop assistant was stacking the shelves.

Richard became quite passionate about the whole project because, like me, he knew it could be good. But by that time it was doomed: I had already lost a lot of money and I told Richard I was going to have to pull the plug soon if things didn't improve. He came up with a whole new set of proposals and I agonized over them all weekend. It was a very tough decision for me to make – it was also my first admission of failure – but on the Monday I called him and told him that it was over. He was very upset, but I think he expected it. In general I am happy to take risks but I have learned that pride and passion have no place in business. Although I really wanted *Bite* to be a success, I had to close it down. Richard broke the news to the team and they were obviously upset, but my decision was final. I had already lost about £1 million on the venture and I wasn't going to waste another penny. The last edition was published in April 1994.

About six months after *Bite* was launched, a member of my staff nominated me, without my knowledge, for the 1993 *Options* magazine 'Women Mean Business' award. I didn't even know about the competition and would not have thought of entering a business award at that time. Anyway, I received this letter from *Options* telling me that I was in the top fifty and was being put forward for the next stage. It was all rather exciting and I agreed to go along for the interview at IPC Magazines.

The first interview was very formal – not at all what I expected. You could have cut the atmosphere with a knife. I also thought I detected a smirk on the judges' faces when they were discussing my business and felt like saying to them: 'What is on your mind?' But by this stage I had committed myself to the competition and couldn't really back out. I was flattered – it was nice to be recognized for my achievements – but somehow I felt uncomfortable about it all. Here I was, Managing Director of my own very successful company, I had just set up *Bite* magazine (and was deep in unhappy negotiations with my own editor), and yet I was sitting being judged by the editor of a magazine, a PR woman and some marketing director of a telecommunications company. Frankly, I did not feel as if I were being judged by my peers.

Despite my concerns, I made it through to the semi-finals and they sent someone down to my office to interview me in detail about the company finances. I had to present the annual accounts and answer some very probing questions. It was all so clinical; there was no opportunity to build up a rapport, no reassurance of confidentiality – nothing to put me at my ease.

I was in a very difficult position. I wanted to do well in the competition not only for myself, but for staff morale, and I didn't want to be seen to be backing down. When *Options* told me I would be notified of their decision in a few weeks, I had already arranged to go on holiday to Thailand. (While I was there the *Daily Express* ran an article saying I had won and quoting me saying how pleased I was!)

Amazingly, in spite of everything, I made it through to the finals. They took place over two days at the Hyde Park Hotel; the final interview was on the first day and the winner was announced on the second. By now I was very apprehensive and I insisted on having a list of the people who were to interview me. The favourites, I learned, were me and Fiona Wright, a lady in the finance industry who had competed last year without success. When I learned that she only employed twelve people and had a much smaller turnover than Ann Summers, I remember thinking, perhaps unfairly, that we weren't really in the same league.

I arrived for the interview and was offered orange juice in this huge ante-room, as if I were an athlete about to enter a marathon. There were two opposing views in my camp: either that, with my sort of business, I didn't stand a chance; or, conversely, that it was in the bag, the award was mine. Not surprisingly, I suppose, the press had looked at the list of finalists and found that, from their point of view, I was the only unusual or noteworthy candidate. With Virginia Bottomley handing out the awards at a time when the Conservatives were going on about Family Values and Back to Basics, who would they rather have standing next to her – a woman who sells sex, or one who markets pension plans? I was, I am afraid, the odds-on favourite.

I had decided to try to take the initiative during the final interview, so I sorted out some information packs about the company with details of the plans and ideas I had put into effect. The big double doors opened and I saw the five judges sitting at a huge boardroom table, with a single seat in front of them for me. I took a deep breath and walked in, smiling. I told them that I had prepared these packs which they might like to look at afterwards and handed them round. They looked at me stony-faced, as if I had just committed some dreadful crime. None of them said a word, so I retreated to the hot seat and the questions started.

The judges comprised the *Options* editor Maureen Price; the previous year's winner – a woman who had set up a cake-making business from home; Susan Woolfe of the boutique chain; and the financial accountant and a director from Hutchison Telecom. The questions came quick-fire. They were hardly allowing each other to finish or me to answer before lining up the next one. Each judge had his or her own agenda, it seemed. There was no time to compose oneself or even to think. It lasted about an hour, but seemed much, much longer.

The one question they kept asking was what my salary was. I told them that I was sorry but it was not a question I was comfortable answering. They seemed embarrassed at first, but then they tried another tack. I didn't see what it had to do with my business acumen. There were lots of questions about the Gold Group, which I thought odd because I assumed I was being judged on my own merits. They were very interested in the other companies and Ann Summers's involvement with them. When I tried to steer the questions back to my business or management philosophy, they persisted in asking about the group.

I was very glad when it was all over, although I felt quite shattered. I had brought Julie, who was incredibly supportive and encouraging and was convinced that I would win. The next day I put on a bright red jacket and skirt and walked into the reception to be greeted by all the reporters and television cameras. The event had attracted tremendous coverage and that, I now realize, was because I was there – the 'sex industry queen', as they like to call me. Everyone was bombarding me with questions and shoving microphones into my face. I was totally taken aback by it all. Although I was accustomed to handling reporters individually, I had never experienced the pack at such close quarters.

Several journalists asked me if I thought Virginia Bottomley would be ordering anything from the catalogue; I said that there was something for everyone and that I would be sending her a copy. Of course that quote was prominently displayed the next day, although I never did receive her order.

There was a photocall in Hyde Park and I was embarrassed because the photographers focused on me all the time; the other finalists were virtually ignored. When it came to the group photo they placed me in the middle and it had started to rain before the individual photos could be taken, so only a very few snaps were taken of the others.

Virginia Bottomley arrived and completely avoided me as I stood giving interview after interview. After her speech the awards were read out. Fiona Wright was the winner. My stomach felt tight with disappointment. Subconsciously I had really hoped that it would be me, partly as a reward for all I had been through and partly for everyone who had supported me. However, I was the runner-up. They called my name and I went up to shake Mrs Bottomley's hand, and you could hear all the cameras clicking away madly and dazzled by the bright television lights. She was meant to stand and pose with me for a few seconds, but she was obviously hating every minute of it and she pulled Fiona Wright between us.

Then I was ushered off the stage and there was another influx of press waiting to interview me and ask how I felt. I was about to try and answer when I saw Julie, looking anxious. She dragged me off to my room. By now I was pretty worried.

She sat me down and said that I wasn't going to like what she was going to tell me. An ex-employee of Ann Summers had telephoned the *Daily Express* and *Options* magazine the previous morning and had said something like: 'Did you know that Ann Summers is part of the Gold Group and Gold Star which publish pornographic magazines?' That wasn't news; all our Party Plan ladies knew about it and we had never tried to hide it. The story had even appeared in several newspapers and I had openly discussed it during interviews. But, at such a moment, it certainly appeared sensational.

The following day the front page of the *Express* showed a picture of me standing with Virginia Bottomley, holding the award; it was accompanied by a short news item. Then a double-page feature appeared the following day with the headline 'TARNISHED GOLD: FAMILY PORNOGRAPHIC EMPIRE THAT LIES BEHIND THE SUCCESS OF ANN SUMMERS BOSS JACQUELINE'. It said of me: 'Don't be fooled by her winning smile and soft dynamism, they mask the family's drive to peddle sexual fantasies to men and women throughout Britain.' It described my father and Ralph as 'the Sultans of Sleaze' and suggested, on the basis of one secretary's complaint, that I did not care for my female staff. I was devastated and took it very personally. Back at the office the calls started flooding in.

I remember wondering how other people in the media spotlight must feel, constantly afraid to open the papers. I look back now and I know that, emotionally, I would handle a situation like that a lot better these days.

It was only much later that I was able to feel good about the whole episode. I see now that it was brave of *Options*, in the face of all the adverse publicity, even to have made me a runner-up. In its way the award represented a great achievement for me. It sits in my office and I am now quite proud of it. The *Options* editor was interviewed on the radio about the competition and she said that when they saw my entry form they laughed – until they saw our annual figures. That, too, was something to be proud of.

The experience toughened me up for something which happened the following year, 1994, when Channel 4 broadcast a documentary about Ann Summers. I thought the programme was very unfair. It all started when a man called Nathan Hartshorn, a television documentary maker, came to see me and asked me if he could do a film about us. Over the years I have been inundated with similar requests and I agreed only because they assured me that the film would be solely about Ann Summers. Although I was aware that it would not be completely pro-Ann Summers, I had been promised that it would be a balanced and positive portrayal.

They spent about fifty hours filming parties and meetings and product launches – all very positive – so everything seemed fine. Then we discovered that they had filmed other events and spoken to other people without consulting us. They had also started to investigate the other companies within the group and to focus on the soft-porn magazines. We then realized that this was not to be a programme solely about Ann Summers after all.

We were in a very difficult position: if we pulled out, we would lose the right to reply and they would run the film anyway. I chose to go ahead because I hoped I would still have some control. When the documentary came out, however, I felt – as did many other people in the industry – that it was very unbalanced. The series was called *High Interest* and our programme was given the title 'Sex in a Cold Climate'. We learned afterwards that, because of the Ann Summers name, the viewing figures rose from 750,000 to 4,000,000 on the Tuesday evening it was shown.

The film struck me as unbalanced because they had filmed three-hour parties where the underwear was the main feature, but had focused entirely on the play products. If you only show part of something, people see it out of context. The games like blowing up a balloon through the legs of the party-goers are a great laugh as part of the overall fun, but if you show them on their own people get the wrong idea. They had also spoken to organizers who had defected to a rival company and were saying things about us that we didn't agree with and were never given a chance to respond to.

I was also annoyed at the way in which they edited the interview

I had given them in the hope of setting the record straight. Asked a key question about the Gold Group, I had stressed that it was like Rupert Murdoch's News International, where *The Times* and the *Sun* and the *News of the World* run completely independently of each other. This answer, which I felt was a vital reply to what they were suggesting, was cut and I felt cheated. I could take no legal action. If we had taken out an injunction to stop it from being broadcast, it would have looked even worse, so we just had to live with it and hope that people understood enough about the media to know that they do not always play fair.

Despite the bad publicity from the *Options* award and Channel 4, in February 1995 I received a letter telling me that I had been chosen as one of the forty finalists in the *Business Age* magazine '40 under 40' awards, which are given every few years to young business people under the age of forty who they think are still going to be successful in ten years' time. I was naturally delighted. At first I did not realize what a prestigious award it was, but I soon discovered that this was very different to the *Options* award as the finalists had already been decided. The panel had gone into it all very thoroughly and I was flattered when I saw that previous winners included Bruce Oldfield and Richard Branson.

They sent someone down to interview me for a short profile; that went well and then I was invited to an awards luncheon. I decided to go: I am not particularly good at networking and this would be a good opportunity. Business lunches are, in my opinion, a waste of time – one always ends up taking three hours to do something one would normally do in one. Recently, however, I have realized that lunches are great for networking – something women are not very good at (men are far better at it, discussing business on the golf course and over breakfast and so on).

I didn't think I would enjoy it but I did. When I left I was given a 'goodie bag' with all sorts of things inside, including a list of the top 500 richest people in Britain. My father and Ralph were about

220th and 222nd: much to Ralph's dismay, my father was about two places ahead of him, which caused some amusement. I think it is calculated in terms of assets and shares, and that year and on those calculations my father was slightly ahead. I think and hope that one day I might be on that list too.

Chapter Eleven
PERSONAL
SERVICES

VERY LITTLE IS known about my father and uncle, the Gold brothers, and people think that this is a deliberate ploy, when actually they are just rather shy and modest. I am amazed by the different attitudes they provoke: some people disapprove totally; most, however, are impressed by their success.

I take after my father in very many ways, and despite the family's wealth, we are both quite modest people with modest tastes. My home is not a palace by any means, and although I do drive a BMW with the personalized number plate A5 LTD (Ann Summers Ltd), I am not extravagant. My father has driven a Daimler for years, and only recently has he moved into a house that really befits his means. For quite some time he lived with Penny in a four-bedroom house in Warlingham. His new home, a beautiful detached Victorian house in Caterham, has become his great love, and it is all we can do to drag him away from it. It needed a massive amount of work but he has turned it into a palace of lovely grand rooms with fireplaces and mirrors (but not on the ceiling!). It has 45 acres of grounds, containing an eight-hole golf course, a swimming pool (complete with the Ann Summers red apple logo in tiles at the bottom), and a floodlit tennis court.

Every year at Christmas when the business closes we all used to go away on holiday as this was the only opportunity for us all to be together – me and Stuart, Vanessa and her boyfriend, my father and Penny, and Ralph. The first Christmas holiday planned was a complete disaster. Ralph's second wife Annie sadly died of cancer, after a long ten-year struggle, so Dad said he would stay behind with Ralph. I left Tony, so Vanessa and her boyfriend ended up going off to Lanzarote on their own. The year after that we went to Puerto Rico, which was great, and we have been to Antigua and Mauritius. However, now that my father has his new house he just wants us to spend Christmas at home.

Holidays are really important to me: I love the sunshine and the indulgence. I suppose it is one area where I am quite extravagant. I enjoy my comforts so I travel first class, stay in really nice hotels, and spend two weeks in total luxury. I don't usually go to the same place twice because I want to see as much of the world as I possibly can and there is not enough time. My favourite so far is Thailand. Stuart and I went in 1993 and it is probably the only place I would return to. I found it fascinating and enchanting.

That holiday started off badly because we went to Egypt first for two days and absolutely hated it. I found the men arrogant and rude and felt oppressed by the constant pestering for money. Stuart and I had not been getting along too well in Cairo, and on the flight to Bangkok we looked in the brochure to discover I had booked the holiday at the height of the rainy season, so we had another row.

But when we arrived we were struck by the contrast: the people were friendly and the hotels were far superior to those in Cairo. We decided to really make the most of our four days there and do all the touristy things, which isn't really our scene, but we had a whale of a time taking boats along the rice canals, going shopping, and visiting the red light district.

There were bars everywhere and men selling tickets to see sex shows, and the whole place was full of tourists, men and women. The atmosphere here was one of entertainment. I was not intimidated as I would have been in Europe and had no sense of the sad and seedy side to a business in which young girls are regularly exploited.

We decided to go in and see one sex show for the experience.

There was a bar with a low stage and male and female tourists were sitting around. For about an hour we watched various incredible acts. One girl fired darts from between her legs at some balloons. Another dropped ping-pong balls into beer glasses from her crotch! One of the acts sticks in my mind because it was so beautiful: it involved a man painting a naked girl. She sat facing us and he painted these exotic flowers on her back in fluorescent paint. When he had finished, she turned round, the lights dimmed and we saw that she was covered in this wonderful art work. I am glad I went and saw it all, although I haven't tried any of the acts at home – not even the balloon/dart routine!

The next stop on our trip was Pattaya. We were a bit dubious about it because we had heard it was the Blackpool of Thailand. But we were booked into the best hotel there, and we had the best of both worlds. We went to a few of the sex shops and shows and had a fantastic night out at a cabaret called Alcatraz. It was a two-hour show featuring men dressed as women. They looked absolutely stunning and sang and danced and did all sorts of acts, all fully clothed. Some had had breast implants and some were on hormones; others were just dressed up, but it was really difficult to tell that they weren't women. A major event in Thailand is an annual beauty show which is televised; the male contestants are shown waiting backstage, as nervous as if they were competing in Miss World. We were open-mouthed as we walked around Pattaya, passing women who were probably really men. Stuart took it all very well, even when he was picked on during one of the shows.

We took a train to the bridge over the River Kwai to visit the war graves and the camps. We also went to an orphanage near our hotel. I love children, despite the fact that I have none of my own, and I was sad to think of them there with no one to love them. The staff were wonderful and showed us around the whole place. They were self-sufficient and kept pigs and chickens. We made a donation when we left.

Last year I went to Singapore and Bali, which everyone had told me was absolutely beautiful, but I found it disappointing – not a patch on Thailand. Singapore was very commercial and clean – just one huge shopping centre after another with all these empty designer shops. I wasn't tempted to buy anything – it was too regimental and formal. I was very interested to see that most of the business people seemed to be female. Well-dressed women hosted business meetings and lunches in the hotels and restaurants, while men were doing menial jobs. Apparently there are a great many single men in Singapore because they do not live up to the high expectations of the women.

When I am on holiday I am a dedicated sunbather – but not *that* dedicated. I want to be as brown as everyone else, but I don't find it easy to relax. Much to Stuart's dismay I have to take my briefcase with me. In my opinion, there is nothing more enjoyable than sitting by the pool with beautiful weather, drinks on tap and my briefcase by my side to dip into.

I love swimming and playing tennis; holidays are the only times when I get the opportunity. After I lost all that weight when I was twenty-six I became more and more interested in healthy eating and the way the body works. I had dieted all my life and knew that my body wasn't functioning very well – when you diet you slow down your metabolism. I had never taken much exercise, so when I started attending classes I noticed the change immediately.

Every now and again I get a craving for sugar, when suddenly I just want a whole packet of biscuits. But I also developed an allergy to certain foods. Grapes and raisins are the worst, although it took me a long time to pinpoint the problem. Raisins, in particular, cause an immediate reaction. I don't drink much alcohol; I can drink wine, but only in small quantities because of the grapes.

I went to an allergy clinic and they put me on an elimination diet, where you eat only four things per week until you get a reaction. They gave me a list of foods I was allergic to. I had identified the raisins myself, but they picked out a few others, like beet sugar, potatoes and malt. With these the reaction is much milder, and I have now been able to reintroduce them into my diet bit by bit. However, I don't think I will ever be able to eat raisins again. No one in my family has food allergies, but funnily enough Stuart is allergic to nuts and seafood. I have to carry an adrenaline injection around for him because if he accidentally ate a nut he could die, which is a terrifying thought.

When I was married I became obsessed with cooking. I was forever preparing wonderfully lavish dinner parties. Tony loved his meat and two veg, but I would never do anything simple like lamb chops – even during the week it was boeuf bourguignon. I was also very competitive: if I went round to a friend's house for dinner and she had made the canapés herself, I felt that I had to do the same. When Tony and I split up and I met Stuart, things changed dramatically. Stuart is a real health-food freak – he will only eat chicken and salad! I remember thinking, 'Gosh, this is easy!' I wanted to fuss and make fancy meals but he wouldn't have any of it because he was quite used to cooking his own meals in the micro-wave. Now I might cook myself something like a jacket potato, but not a proper dinner or anything substantial. I simply do not have the time, and even if I did, nowadays I want to do more with my life than be tied to the kitchen sink.

Consequently, I do eat out a lot. For everyday meals, I have someone at home to cook meals for my freezer - so many per week – so that I can just come in and pop one in the microwave. I usually have a pasta dish or something with rice or potatoes – I don't eat very much meat. Vanessa is much more homey than me and cooks a lovely Sunday roast. Her partner cooks as well; they are both quite domesticated.

Now I go to a local gym between three and five times a week and I love it. I had a personal trainer for about three years, but my work schedules meant that I was forever cancelling at the last minute, and I found it very pressured. I ended up not really enjoying it, so I started going to step aerobics classes instead and, for the first time ever, I was finding exercise fun. Now, if I cancel I don't feel guilty, although I very rarely miss a class and I am really disappointed if my work commitments prevent me from attending. I go with my friend Lorraine and we have a great time. There is quite a skill to step aerobics, and it is very good exercise, particularly when you feel you are in competition with your class mates and don't want to lag behind.

I take great personal pride in my appearance and have my hair and fingernails done regularly, although I don't find it a treat. Having a manicure is the most boring experience for me: you can't read or make a telephone call or do anything but sit there. As for my hair, I am very particular who I go to now. I had a disaster with it a few years ago and vowed never to make the same mistake again.

I don't really have time for hobbies any more, but I love fashion shows, especially the big name ones, and I do try to fit in a few each year. My favourite colour is red. I think it is a passionate colour, warm and approachable.

I love the theatre, especially the musicals, and have been to quite a few, including *Miss Saigon*, *Grease* and *Carousel*. I also go to the cinema a couple of times a month, if possible. Occasionally I hire a video to watch at home.

My habits have changed quite a lot over the years. In the early days I loved gardening and cooking and sewing and all the homey things. I have even sewn tapestries. The one I am most proud of hangs in my hallway. It is a country scene with sheep and meadows and an embroidered mount. It took me ages to finish it, and although it is a kit, it was not marked out and was very much a matter of personal interpretation and design. I really enjoyed making it, although I can't imagine doing it now. I tend to go through a phase of liking something and then dropping it because I lose interest and I want to go on and try something else.

For a while I used to do watercolours. I would paint animals, or flowers or pretty cottage scenes. I haven't picked up a paintbrush in years but I have always had an artistic flair. Vanessa is creative, but she expresses it in her approach to life. She is a very good cook, but her chief hobby as a teenager was potholing. I once tried riding, but it was a disaster from start to finish. The horse would spot me a mile away and think, 'I am going to have her!' I would always end up on the ground with a bruised bottom.

My house is very neat and tidy. I don't like lots of clutter. I will see something I really like and think, 'Where can I put that?'; if there is a spot for it I will buy it, otherwise I won't. I am never deliberately extravagant when it comes to my home – I don't buy things just for the sake of buying them.

I spend a lot of money on security, which I feel is important for a woman living alone, but obviously not enough because my BMW cabriolet was stolen from the driveway under my very nose. I have an alarm system, a video camera and sensors, as well as electric garage doors, but now I am planning to get electric gates and a wall. I have top-of-the-range locks and security but, as the police told me after my car was stolen, if someone is determined to get in, they will.

I don't really collect anything in particular, although I have bought quite a few pictures over the years. I brought back a parchment picture from Egypt and another painting from Thailand. One of my favourites is one of three prints I had of woodland scenes with little animals in it which I had as a child. I had added a few extra animals in pencil, but I was able to erase them before I framed and hung them in the spare bedroom. I also have two really lovely prints I bought last year when I was in San Diego for the DSA conference. One is of two huge polar bears, a mother and baby, in the snow. The other is of three grizzly bears, a mother and her two babies, by a river. They were quite expensive but I have no regrets because I love them.

If my house was on fire, I think the first thing I would grab would be my favourite coat, which one of my previous cleaning ladies once stole (but which the police found hanging up in her wardrobe when I reported it missing). It was a very expensive impulse buy and I feel I have been through so much with it. There are also some photographs that mean a lot to me – the one of me and the Beatles, one of me and Vanessa, and another very precious one of me and my father taken when I was quite little. I am just standing there in a little navy blue hat and coat. I don't remember my father and I being together very often when I was young, but in this picture he looks so proud of me and me of him. I sometimes think, if I knew then what I know now . . .

Over the years, at home as well as at work, I have evolved the philosophy that if you can get other people to do something, then you should so that you can save your time and energy for things you are good at. Generally speaking, I have been very lucky with the people I have employed. My gardener, Maija, has been working for me for years. She is Swedish and I first met her when I was living with Tony in Chaldon and I advertised for a gardener there. All these men turned up and then she came along; I hadn't expected a woman. She is very tall and animated, and she had so much enthusiasm for gardening that I took her on. After I split up with Tony, it was about three years before I moved to a house with a garden. I had kept her number, so I rang her and was delighted to find that she was still there. She has worked for me ever since.

She really takes care of the garden and I give her a completely free hand. Every now and again she leaves me a list of problems we need to discuss and we make an appointment. Each year she fills my window boxes with geraniums and they look stunning. I don't have much time to enjoy the garden, but on a hot summer's day I love sitting on the patio in the sun having my breakfast.

I am quite houseproud and I'm a compulsive cushion-plumper; if someone turns up unexpectedly and I haven't plumped my cushions, I think, 'Oh my God it looks so untidy!' My wonderful housekeeper, Doreen, has worked for me for years and has become a very important part of my life. She reminds me of Dorothy, Tony's mother: she is about the same age, with the same warm, bubbly personality. She runs the house beautifully for me – everything is always just the way I like it. She was the first lady I interviewed when I advertised for someone in the local paper, so I was extremely lucky. She comes in every day except weekends and does all the ironing and shopping; if there are workmen coming or anything like that, she will let them in and supervise them.

I trust Doreen implicitly and she is very caring and thoughtful. She and I have become very fond of each other and she proudly collects all my newspaper clippings and follows my career closely. I have to save any new articles for her so that she doesn't miss anything. I really appreciate her support, especially when I remember my uncle Ralph's cleaning lady, who resigned in disgust after reading an article about his publishing empire in the *Daily Telegraph* in the 1970s.

Early in 1995 I came home one day to find a note from Doreen, which had obviously been written under great stress. It said: 'Jacky, I am really sorry, I can't work for you again. I have just found out I have cancer. I am sorry. Doreen.' It was almost as if she expected me to say, 'OK, then I will get someone else in'; she obviously didn't realize how much I cared for her. I went round to see her and she told me what had happened. She had had cancer ten years ago, at the same time as her sister was diagnosed as having breast cancer. Doreen had a hysterectomy and survived, but her sister had left it too late.

In November 1994 she found a lump in her neck but she didn't go to the doctor until January, two months later. They performed a biopsy and found that it was cancer and said that the lump had to be removed. She was told that she would have to have her voice-box removed, which was really devastating news for her. I desperately wanted to help, but in the end all I could do was give her my support. I let her know that her job was there if she wanted it, but that she was under no pressure to return. Instead of getting a replacement, I used agency cleaners until she was well enough to make a decision. They were hopeless compared to Doreen: every week there seemed to be another breakage or disaster.

Doreen has a husband and two grown-up children, who have

been very supportive, but I was delighted when she asked for my help. She is very gentle and was worried about the operation but was afraid to ask her doctor about it. I said, 'Why not let me ask for you?' and rang the hospital, pretending to be her daughter so that I could get some answers for her. I had to be pretty assertive and pushy before they told me what I wanted to know, and they were quite stroppy with me at first, so I hope Doreen's daughter didn't get into trouble when she later visited her mother there.

After the operation I wanted to go and visit her in hospital, but her husband said she was too embarrassed to see me. I went to see her at home later and she was coping well. The doctors seem to be very optimistic about her progress. They put her on radium treatment – which seemed to be more of a formality than anything else – and she was soon back at work. She obviously had to learn new communication skills, which was very difficult for her, and what worried me most was how her wonderful confidence would suffer. It was a terrible start to my year, and came at a time when I had just suffered another shock.

In December 1994, when I was in the midst of the build-up to Christmas and the 1995 Annual Conference, I had an emotional telephone call from Derek to tell me that Dorothy had had a heart attack and had been rushed to hospital. Ever since I was married to Tony, Dorothy and Derek have always looked upon me as the daughter they never had. When he told me what had happened, I just couldn't believe it. Dorothy had seemed so healthy and fit and full of life. She swims every day and follows a low-fat diet and is very slim. Although both her parents suffered fatal heart attacks, her father when he was forty, it had never occurred to me – or anyone else – that she would have one. She was in her early sixties and she had been there for me almost all my life.

Derek told me she had woken in the night with what she thought was a bad case of indigestion. Without waking him up, she had gone downstairs to take an indigestion tablet, but found that she was in too much pain to swallow it. She sat there for a few hours until Derek woke and came down to see what was the matter. He wanted to call the doctor, but she said no and this argument went on all night. Eventually he prevailed, and the doctor who examined her diagnosed a heart attack.

At this stage, Derek said, she was looking greyer and greyer and the doctor had her taken to the local hospital. He told me that he hadn't rung Tony because Dorothy didn't want him to worry, and I realized that I was the first person he had called. Tony had to be told, I said, but he didn't want to let Dorothy down. In the end I telephoned her at the hospital to get her OK. Derek still seemed very emotional so I said: 'Do you want me to do it?' and he said: 'Would you?' and I called Tony to explain what had happened. I remember him asking why they had rung me first, but I told him it was just that I was the first person they thought of, and that they didn't want to worry him, and he accepted that. He knew how much his parents thought of me and me of them.

Tony and I arranged to go down and see them. He went first and I flew down to Newquay Airport a couple of days later. I spent the day there and Derek and I went out to lunch. When I flew back home, having seen Dorothy, I felt a lot happier. Then, two days later, Derek called to tell me she'd had another heart attack. Fortunately, she was in good hands and she pulled through, but it warned me of the dangers of complacency.

I think Dorothy's heart attack was caused by worry. They had just moved house and had the workmen in and there was a lot to organize. She is a bit like me: everything has to be just so. In hospital she worried about Derek, who is diabetic, although very sporty and fit (he is a judo instructor). It was ironic that they had moved because of Derek's health, yet it was Dorothy who became ill.

I went back to see her and she looked very tired. Tony was constantly on the phone to me, suggesting that we should sort out the house and the workmen for them. Dorothy would only listen to me, he said. My advice to him was that we should offer them our help and let them decide what they wanted to do. It was easy to move in and take over their lives, but it might not be the best thing. You can do too much in such situations.

Tony and I had always kept in touch since our marriage break-up, but since Dorothy's illness I have always been ready to offer my support and advice on what to do about his parents, whom I love dearly. Dorothy now jokes about something I said to her at the time. I was asking whether she thought she might get a cleaning lady in a few days a week and apparently I told her: 'Don't worry about whether or not she'll be suitable. I'll fly down for the day and interview her.' She had visions of this poor cleaning lady, working for just a few pounds an hour, shaking in her shoes because this managing director of a multi-million-pound company was going to fly down for the day and ask her if she would do the ironing!

This was my first contact with serious illness and it panicked me; I know it panicked Tony. I feel very thankful that Doreen and Dorothy have both recovered so well. When my maternal grandmother was alive and her siblings died off one by one, she reacted less and less as she became more and more immune to the grief of it all. I suppose it is nature's way of coping, but I can't imagine ever feeling like that.

Chapter Twelve
A GOLDEN FUTURE

OROTHY'S HEART attack had a traumatic effect on me. At that time I was under a great deal of pressure at work and I suddenly found myself feeling really ill. I couldn't sleep at night for palpitations and a burning feeling in my chest. The pains would run down both arms, down my back and into my spine. Then I felt unable to breathe, as if I was having warm water poured over my head.

I am the sort of person who can scare herself very easily, and I was afraid to go to sleep in case I didn't wake up again. I even felt as if I were having a heart attack myself. Eventually I went to the doctor's and they strapped this heart monitor to me for a couple of days, which was very uncomfortable and made me even more worried.

It was at this time that Loretta Leese died and I had to get up terribly early in the morning to travel to Derby for her funeral. The night before I had had one of my attacks, and had got less than two hours' sleep. I drove up there feeling awful. The service was very emotional and moving and suddenly I started to suffer the same symptoms that I had previously only had at night. As I stood there I felt so stifled and ill I thought I was going to black out. I rushed away as soon as I decently could and went straight back to the doctor that evening to ask what it was.

He said there was nothing seriously wrong with me, I was just suffering from stress brought on by all that was going on in my life. He said I was hyperventilating and having anxiety attacks and then making matters worse by scaring myself into thinking I was having a heart attack. I was so relieved to hear that I was all right, and somehow knowing that made me feel better. Within a few weeks, once the Annual Conference was over, I felt very much better and I am delighted to say that the symptoms have completely disappeared.

Looking back, I should have known that at some time in my busy life I was going to suffer from some of the recognized symptoms of stress; it is very common in people with jobs like mine. I hope that in the future I will be able to control it better and take time out to compensate for the fast corporate pace.

I sometimes think that I could almost cut my life in two. Before my success at Ann Summers I was much quieter – even timid – and allowed myself to be dominated by other people. Then I suddenly became a completely different person. I have to pinch myself sometimes when I realize that I now head this vast organization of thousands of women holding nearly 5,000 parties a week, and that Ann Summers, with a gross annual turnover of around £40 million, ranks among the top 200 most profitable registered private companies in the UK. It seems a very long way from Thamesmead and that smoky little room.

In achieving that success I've had to break out of various restricting stereotypes. Men have very definite ideas of how a woman in business should look and behave, particularly when she is fronting an operation in the sex industry. I have had to jump over a lot of hurdles in my career – being a woman was just one of the biggest. But with each year that goes by many women – not just me – are establishing their professional and personal needs.

Writing this book has helped to bring things into perspective in many ways and has made me feel even closer to the people I love. Looking through old photographs and going over old memories with my mother, for example, has made me understand her better. I see now that she was probably never quite as strong as I imagined her to be. It is only in recent years that she tells me that she is proud of me. In the early days she would never say — and I would never ask. We are very warm towards each other now.

I know I am unusual because I have never felt broody. I like children, but I don't often come into contact with them. I think I would make a good mother. I have a very clear idea of how I would bring up children of my own. To start with, there would be no shortage of love — not suffocating love, but a warm, open love, and I would try to reason with them. If they did something wrong and I had to tell them off, I would try to explain why. I would also resist being too gooey and spoiling them. The only trap I might fall into — one that I would be very wary of — is being over-protective. You have to allow children the freedom to go off and play or stay the night with friends or they will feel trapped and stifled, as I did. The difficulty is in getting the balance right.

The thought of having children is sometimes appealing. When I am older I may well look back and regret not having any. But I feel I am at the peak of my career. There is still so much that I want to do. I enjoy being spontaneous and doing things as and when I want, without having to worry about responsibilities. I think it is unrealistic for people to say, 'Oh well, you can get a nanny and carry on working.' Having children changes your life dramatically; I would not give up work so there would have to be compromises, which I would hate.

Meanwhile, running Ann Summers and keeping it healthy and growing gives me no time to reflect on such matters. There are always new challenges and new battles to fight. Our most recent problem was similar to the troubles we faced with Silver Rose and Lovelace, and involved a company called Intrigue. It started in August 1994 when they began poaching some of our ladies, taking some 200 away from us. Their adverts even said: 'Ann Summers girls wanted.' I tried to clamp down on this; apparently *they* were allowed to say that, but the newspapers were not allowed to print it, so I stopped them running the ads. Set up by the Texas group, a huge engineering conglomerate, Intrigue became a threat when they were joined by an ex-Ann Summers area manager called Philippa Clayburn, who had left us some time ago. They guaranteed our ladies company cars and no targets to lure them away, and the sort of tactics I had seen used twice before.

The senior ladies that left had all been with us a long time, and joined before we introduced the new contracts which compel them to hand over their lists of customers and hostesses. I knew that Intrigue must have taken some of these lists from the senior staff, but it was very difficult to obtain the necessary evidence. Effectively, they were getting all the organizers and telephone numbers for free, without even having to provide any training. They were simply setting up a company on the back of Ann Summers.

Solicitor's letters were sent to them threatening legal action, but Intrigue claimed these ladies were all known to them as friends. I was at a loss, but then one of their employees called me and said he had something to tell me. He came to see me with what he said was inside information about the way in which the company planned to progress. Some of this information was obviously exaggerated, and it was very difficult for me to tell what was genuine. Eventually, without any help from him, I managed to get hold of the evidence I needed to prove that Intrigue had in their possession some private Ann Summers documents. One of the ex-area managers had sent letters to the ladies she was poaching for Intrigue actually using our labels but cutting the edges off the corners, which showed their old Ann Summers account number. The letters began: 'Hi there! I am not poaching you . . .'! We were able to match up the labels and the font and prove that this was Ann Summers property. My solicitor and I were both ecstatic.

In March 1995 I was preparing for a full-scale battle and was about to approve the affidavit and injunction to stop this company when we heard that they had gone into receivership. I was delighted, although I was ready with my gloves off this time.

These days I am much tougher and more determined to fight to the bitter end for what we have achieved. I would even use private detectives if I thought it would help – anything that I can do legally to stop the raids on our company. Our experiences have helped us to develop better action plans. We have to make sure we protect our company against copycats and that we do it quickly. We have trademarks and copyrights on every aspect of our business now, and anyone who wants to take us on better have a fat legal budget.

We are, of course, vulnerable because of the nature of the system and the girls that we rely on. Party Plan is a very complex business that requires a great deal of organization and infrastructure. We have been threatened by only three rivals in fourteen years, which isn't bad going, and all three have ended up the worse off. I could have predicted the outcome in every case. We just have to try to learn from these experiences and wait until another one bites the dust. None of them pose a long-term threat to us, although they are a nuisance in the short term.

You need a lot of money behind you to set up a Party Plan organization. When I started I had a loan from the board of the modern equivalent of about £150,000 to get it going, and I was also able to use the resources of this huge distribution and publishing empire.

The 200 ladies we lost to Intrigue could almost have represented a whole area (we have fifteen areas in the country). Luckily they took girls from different areas, but some, like Manchester, were hit very badly. It is not only the ladies we lose, of course, but their recruiting power.

Julie Harris was brilliant through all of this. She organized a seminar and invited the ladies who had defected by advertising in the paper and telling them that Intrigue had gone bust. About fifty of the 200 turned up – not a huge number, but more than we managed to woo back from Lovelace. The *Manchester Evening News*, which ran the advert, sent a reporter along to the seminar and published an article about it, which was an added bonus.

A few days after the seminar I went to an area meeting in Nottinghamshire, one of the areas affected, where I really wanted to make an impact. I had been told a funny story about Intrigue and decided to tell it to the audience exactly as it was told to me. I didn't want to shy away from what had happened; I wanted to share my concerns in a light-hearted way, and my speech went something like this:

> You will be delighted to hear that Intrigue has gone into receivership [big round of applause], but there is a very interesting story circulating which I am sure you haven't heard. You know that the Gold Group, which owns Ann Summers, owns half of the *Sport* newspaper. Intrigue apparently did *not* know because when they went into receivership and were looking to get rid of some of their stock, they decided to contact the *Sport* and see if they could offload it through a reader offer. The girl who took the call listened to all that they had to say and then replied: 'You obviously don't know that Ann Summers owns half of the *Sport*, so you can piss off!'

We have always been a company run by women for women and that ethos still applies in the 1990s. Of our nearly 300 employees, only a few are men, and, I am delighted to have them on board and am grateful for their input. Two of them, my Merchandising Executive and Finance Executive, are key members of my core team.

It has taken me a long time to get my key team right because I was determined not to make any mistakes. It is a bit like playing tennis: if you play with someone better than you, you perform better yourself.

When Ann Summers started we obviously used the existing GGI accounts structure, but we reached the stage where that system just wasn't adequate any more and I felt I needed to bring in my own people. My team are all so progressive and forward think-

ing with a wealth of ideas. I love that type of energy and enthusiasm. In a business which is very steady it is easy to get set in your
ways, but Party Plan isn't like that. It cannot survive by doing today
what it did yesterday and the day before. We are constantly looking
to change.

Although we always had a personnel function within the group,
it was purely procedural and I realized that we needed someone of
our own. Everyone was against me employing such a person. They
thought that personnel meant redundancies and disciplinary procedures and getting rid of people. Management were also against it
because they regarded it as a time-wasting 'tea and sympathy' role.
But they were proved wrong. I had lots of ideas on what I wanted to
implement and the person I took on board was able to help.

I have now restructured the business by reshaping certain areas,
such as the sharing of functions like accounts and transport and
computing within the group. When we were growing so fast we
didn't always have the time to do the right thing; when there was a
problem I sometimes sent in the wrong person. When he or she
then failed it was very demotivating for the team, and it wasn't necessarily that person's fault. Fortunately I was able to put things
right without upsetting the apple-cart too much. Where people
were out of their depth we have helped them, without demoting or
demotivating them, through utilizing their key strengths. I now try
to get my key staff to pick the right people in the first place so that
we are not put in that position.

Of course we do make people redundant. I am not the sort of
person who believes in having surplus staff whether we are doing
well or not. Fortunately, we haven't had to do it too often over the
years, and we do have a policy of redeploying people where possible
– if not in Ann Summers then elsewhere within the group. I have
fired many people – in some instances for stealing from us – and I
have no difficulty with that at all, but making someone redundant
is sad. Some redundancies I have handled personally, others I
haven't, but I am always directly involved. My stance is, firstly, can

we redeploy? If the person is too senior or too specialized it can be difficult. I treat each case individually.

My father and I are very much on the same wavelength, but making staff changes is the one area where I really do have to bully him. He is a softie and I love him dearly, but when it comes to sacking people who are no longer right for the company, he would rather just keep paying them to do nothing until they retire or choose to leave. I am quite different in that respect. No matter how sweet someone is or how loyal they have been, if they are holding the company back I don't hesitate to ask them to leave. I think too many bosses are afraid of the disciplinary procedures and settlement arrangements and do not use them as they should be used. I regard them as tools which allow us to put things right, not as a hindrance to achieving our goals.

There are people who meet me socially and wonder how this quietly spoken individual can control a multi-million-pound empire. If you spoke to my staff, however, they would have no hesitation in dismissing that misconception. I would never deliberately upset people but I always have and always will put the success of Ann Summers first. And if I come across as ruthless, then so be it! However, many, many of my staff have been with me for over ten years. I do try to cultivate a work environment that makes everyone happy, and I hope that it works. I always think something through very carefully first; I don't go bulldozing my away around and treading on everyone in sight. I am much more quietly manipulative.

I am a very change-orientated person. Some people believe in the saying: 'If it is not broken, don't fix it,' but I believe in forward thinking and preparing for the unexpected. My father is reluctant to change and I have to bully him about it sometimes. He thinks I am very bossy but believe me, I have had to be. I am the one person who can really challenge him, and because he knows that I wouldn't even suggest something to him unless I thought it was right, I do generally get my way. Dad is very approachable, but he has some

'Yes' people around him who are afraid to speak their minds simply because of who he is. I actively encourage people to say what is on their minds – it's the only way to move forward. I like to be challenged and questioned and put on the spot.

I think my father and I have both learned a lot from each other. He is very aware of the importance of motivating staff, but I think that he is not so good when it comes to giving criticism, even when it is constructive. We certainly have the same view on pay and rewards and giving the best people the salaries and packages they deserve. That is very important in a big company like ours. Key members of the team, who are directly influencing the company and the profits, should naturally be rewarded.

Of course the organizers' pay rises as the prices of the items they sell go up. Our main aim is to make sure the quality people come through to manager level. I am constantly reviewing the area manager structure: it has been based on salary plus commission and expenses, but will probably become purely commission-based. This move has been well received by the senior people so far: it will enable the high-achievers to substantially increase their salaries and virtually run their own business with their own budgets and everything. They currently earn up to about £30,000 a year, but under the new system they could earn in the region of £40,000–£45,000 a year, which makes us much more competitive and gives those lower down the scale something to aim for, although the non-achievers won't be happy because they will no longer be carried by the system.

I try to be as realistic as possible about salaries. It would be foolish of me to decide to give myself a 400 per cent rise just because I felt like it. Pay and rewards must be based on sound commercial sense and on the value of that person to the company. My salary is decided by myself and the board and is based on the current financial situation. It is something I will not reveal: it is my business and no one else's. (I think one of the reasons we have never floated Ann Summers on the Stock Market – although many people have asked us to consider it — is because we want to remain in control of our business. Also, incidentally, we don't need the money.)

Some journalist once wrote in an article that I earned £250,000 a year, which was not true, and I was concerned because people tend to believe what they read in newspapers. Since then I have often been portrayed as 'one of the highest earning female executives in the country', which I find rather odd as no one outside the company knows what I earn. The *Daily Mail* recently placed me forty-seventh in a league of Britain's highest earning women, claiming I paid myself £432,000 a year. I was, apparently, two places above Ulrika Jonsson and five down from Joanna Lumley!

I am looking forward to becoming the chairperson of the Gold Group. It will probably be the greatest challenge I have ever faced. I have always maintained a healthy interest in the group and although I don't have too much time to spend on it I am familiar with how it all works and know which companies are doing better than others and so on. The same business principles apply; it is just a different product. I don't think it will be too hard taking overall control. There are obviously a lot of changes I would like to make, but I am not impulsive; I will bide my time.

First and foremost my commitment is to Ann Summers and its continuing expansion. It is not all wine and roses: 1994 saw a slight drop in profits and a minimal faltering of growth, but that was caused mainly by perfidious competition and by our losses on *Bite*, both now behind us. It keeps us on our toes, in any case, and makes us realize that we can't afford to be complacent. There is always room for improvement: I have some exciting plans in the pipeline. Our growth in Europe is an area which I will be concentrating on in the short term. I am researching a whole new product range and concept which will interest men! But the most time consuming project on my business plan at present will ensure guaranteed growth for Ann Summers . . . but I'm not prepared just yet to divulge further details. You will have to 'watch this space' as they say!

One of our biggest challenges recently has been to implement our plan to refurbish all our old shops and open up several new ones spearheaded by GGI director Patrick Harold. It is part of a £2 million scheme to break into the High Street. The Charing Cross shop, as the flagship, was the first. We moved it to a better site two doors along and the shop was redesigned to match the more sophisticated Ann Summers profile, which has attracted a new type of customer. Sales are well above the predicted targets. Southampton, Croydon, and Queensway are doing well too. The shops provide an outlet for men and couples who, more and more, like to choose purchases together.

I am constantly surprised and delighted by the success of Ann Summers and by the public interest in the woman who runs it. The idea of a book about Ann Summers never appealed to me at all, even when Kim Waterfield tried to talk me into it. It was only when a number of publishers approached me some years later that I realized that perhaps people were interested in my story.

People seem to be fascinated with how a nice girl like me came to be running a business like this. If ever I wanted to give up running Ann Summers, I could have a career as a public speaker. After the *Options* award I was inundated with requests from charities and other organizations to speak at their conferences. It was a new experience for me, so I decided to do a few and I really quite enjoyed it. One conference I attended was for business women. There were three other speakers – a woman politician, the editor of a home magazine and a Canadian representative from the Salvation Army. The woman politician was, I thought, very boring and talked about Sunday trading; the editor was incredibly nervous; but the Canadian was absolutely brilliant, better than any of us. Her presentation about battered wives and women who turn to prostitution really captured my attention. She spoke very well and had a lovely accent and I felt such admiration for her. Watching other women speak and hearing about their successes or failures was fascinating. I have learned over the years that it is all down to two things: confidence and experience.

I try to gain everyone's attention and build a rapport by walking into the audience and getting them to take part. Sometimes I ask everyone to put both their hands in the air and reach as high as they can; then I ask them to reach a bit higher, and higher still. There is always at least one person who stands up on a chair or on the table – it is a great demonstration of how people can always reach that little bit further if you ask them to; some will have the sense to use what is around them to help them up. I also have a routine where I ask people to fold their arms and then ask them quickly to fold them the other way. It is a way of showing how difficult it is to accept change. Each speech I give is tailor-made to the event, but I tend to draw on the same themes.

The last one I did was for Meals on Wheels, whose conference theme was 'Food Is Fun'. I was amazed when they asked me to speak. A lady came to see me at Gadoline House. I gave her a tour round the building and afterwards she was still very keen for me to go. She said they were trying to be more commercial and competitive and wanted someone successful and dynamic to inspire them. I asked her lots of questions about the members and found out that they were mainly women, almost all elderly, and all volunteers. Meals on Wheels is the largest voluntary organization in the UK; they are facing many changes and are not finding it easy to adapt.

I realized I had a really tough job on my hands because I was used to dealing with people who were motivated by money and I wondered how I was going to be able to link my success to theirs. Anyway, off I went to Birmingham. When I arrived they were all eating lunch. I walked into that room in my suit and saw all these blue-rinsed little old ladies dining in their green matron-type uniforms sitting down to their roast and I thought I had made a terrible mistake.

I sat down amongst them, and they were all extremely warm and friendly to me. I remember thinking: 'Oh my God, they don't know what Ann Summers is!' and I began to get cold feet. If what I said didn't go down very well, I decided, I would try something different. I went up to the microphone for a photocall with the senior volunteers and then all the ladies came in and sat down waiting for me to speak. This was to be the highlight of their day. It was a long time since I had been so apprehensive.

As I launched into my speech I started to relax. The secrets of my success, I told them, were perseverance, hard work and determination. I asked how many of them had passed their driving test first time. Many of them raised their hands. Then I ask how many passed second time, and a few more hands went up. Finally, I asked how many people passed their driving test the third time, and at this point I raised my own hand. I told them that those who had failed several times succeeded in the end because they were determined.

Then I gave them another example. I asked them to put their hands up if they could remember their first sexual experience, which brought a smile to many faces. A few people laughed and said it was so long ago they couldn't remember. I raised my own hand and then I asked them what it was like and, using a roving microphone, I sought out the people whose hands were up and they gave me their answers, some of which were hilarious. By now everyone was giggling. A few of the hands went down as soon as I approached them with the mike, but I teased them into replying. Most of us, I went on, if we are really honest, will admit that our first sexual experience was terrible. But none of us give up because of that bad experience, and we all keep going until we get it right. Everyone laughed and I had a very enthusiastic reception.

I also told them about the Love Seat and the man who wrote to me about its possible marketing and that also went down well. At the end the senior people asked them if they had any questions to ask me, and they were wonderful. One woman looked at my suit and asked if I could design the new uniforms for Meals on Wheels, and an old boy stood up and said he would like to know if Meals on Wheels would be introducing Ann Summers's edible undies into the meals range. That took me quite by surprise and received a tremendous laugh. I said they were very welcome to, but I didn't think they would be terribly nutritious.

I learned something very important at that lunch: that I had had preconceived ideas of my own about these people which had nearly made me back out of speaking to them. Suddenly I realized that I was doing to them what people had done to me for years by assuming that they knew what I was like either because of the way I looked or because of what I did. It was a very useful experience and I now advise my organizers not to have preconceptions about others and to take people as they find them.

Some people reading this book might think I have not shown them the hard edge that I must secretly possess to have been so successful in such a male-dominated business as the sex industry. But, in many ways, it is precisely because it has been so male-dominated for so long that my softer, more feminine approach has won the day.

I pride myself on surprising those with preconceptions of how someone like me should be. I am simply not the hard-faced, brassy bitch that many people automatically assume me to be.

In many ways I am much more devious than that. I deliberately seek to manipulate situations to my own advantage by using my persuasive guile, rather than by forcing the day. Like the thousands of women who are our customers and organizers, I know that the best way to get what you want from men is to manoeuvre them into thinking that whatever you had in mind was their idea in the first place.

I hope that I have proved that women can now make a success of their lives without the compromises that so many have previously had to make. Forget the power dressing, the spectacles and the severe hairstyles or – at the other end of the scale – plunging cleavages and the need to flirt with the middle managers.

There is a middle ground and it requires nothing but honesty and femininity and the ability to be confident in yourself and to openly employ all the assets at your disposal to get what you want, be it a winning smile or a reasoned insistence. That is how I have got to the top and, perhaps because I was in a business which least expected it, it is also what keeps me there.

I certainly hope that I have shattered a few myths and dispelled a few assumptions about myself. If there is a message to be found in my success and that of Ann Summers, it is that nothing in life should be taken too seriously. First and foremost, Ann Summers is about having fun – how to have fun yourself and how to help others rediscover fun for themselves. As someone once said somewhere, you can be forgiven for your happiness and your success, if you generously consent to share them. I have enjoyed sharing them with you.

I want to receive information about joining Ann Summers

Name: ....Miss/Mrs/Ms

Address: ....

....

....

Town: ....County: ....

Postcode: ....Telephone No: ....

Date: ....

Signature: ....

Please send to: Ann Summers
Press Office
Gadoline House
2 Godstone Road
Whyteleafe
Surrey CR3 0EA
Tel: 0181 660 0102

To book a party or order a catalogue telephone: 0181 660 7129